Testimonials

I heartily endorse the messages in *Refractive Thinker, Volume XI: Women and Leadership*. Working as a teacher in public education, I appreciate the dedication of the authors of the excellent research contained in this anthology, towards helping women realize their career goals promote equity, and share their talents in helping each other rise to the challenges of leadership.

Leah Lehrburger, *Elementary Music Teacher, Teacher of the Year Candidate for Douglas County School District, Colorado*

In an enlightening discussion, Dr. Aaron and Dr. Cheryl capture the heart of the issues surrounding gender defined leadership and encourage us to find a better definition that is independent of traditional and limiting stereotypes of gender, race, and age.

Leanne Donoghue-Tamplin, *Australian Psychologist and Coach,* www.realsuccess.com.au

This is an excellent book that is packed with peer reviewed research. I enjoyed the thoughts from the academic entrepreneur at the end of each chapter.

Jason Boyd, *Senior Environmental Health Specialist*

Once again, Dr. Cheryl Lentz has gathered a brilliantly astute group of authors. This time the goal was to illustrate and demonstrate the necessary assertion that women need to be more involved in the planning and decisions being made determining the health of the global economy and security as well as the overall stability of our planet.

Elizabeth Phinney, *Creator of BodSpir (fitnessafterfortyfive.com), Consultant, Trainer, Author, Speaker*

This eleventh issue of *The Refractive Thinker* Anthology Series contains a refreshing set of relevant and applied research contributions to traditional networking and leadership topics in the context of female leaders and how to overcome the gender bias within an organization. As a Financial Controller, I enjoyed reading about Dr. Boese's findings related to the potential of female accountants and the role of educational institutions to empower women in pursuing a career in Finance.

Dr. René Puls, *Business Researcher & Head of Corporate Controlling (Oil & Gas Downstream)*

This is a timely beautifully written collaborative book, and a must read for women in any age and profession, each leader and aspiring leader. The book and its chapters highlight the historical evolvement of women in leadership positions, leaving the reader with new ideas about the role of higher education and leadership development for women as a form of public good. The tools presented are useful as research topics for Master's and Doctoral programs. I would highly recommend the assignment of the book in women studies, leadership studies, and other academic settings.

Dr. Denis Mayo-Moore takes the point of leadership success. What are the tools and methodologies for success? One very important question is how we develop leadership, during childhood especially for young girls. This book will leave the reader with the question who will be the role model of leadership for young girls, and will provide a way to look at this question with solutions in mind.

Edith Neumann, PhD, *Provost and Chief Academic Officer of Touro University Worldwide*

After reading *The Refractive Thinker*, I am struck by the clarity and focus of the study of women in leadership roles. I know it is difficult as the definition of gender roles has continued to play a large part in a child's upbringing and all through their formative years. Identifying leaders no matter where they are will help to create future leaders, based on qualities not stereotypes.

As a mother of two very successful daughters and personally as a business owner, licensed contractor and designer, becoming an expert in my industry and respected as a leader in a male dominated field has been a challenge, but ultimately very satisfying journey.

Karen Holt, *ConservationScholars.org*

One of the most heartbreaking occurrences I observed during my 30 years in higher education was the failure of students to complete doctoral programs due to their inability to write and defend dissertations. There are many reasons why half of all doctoral students fail to complete the dissertation.

That said, I find myself agreeing with Dr. Kathi Gibson that the lack of adequate mentoring is clearly at the top of the list! Dr. Gibson has seen the problem from every perspective imaginable and her insights and experiences give valuable guidance to those with responsibility to change the status quo. Universities need to recognize and address the need to better mentor all students, but especially women, so that they can clear the dissertation hurdle and assume higher levels of responsibility and authority in their chosen fields.

Leonard O. Pellicer, *Distinguished Professor Emeritus, University of South Carolina*

An amazing and thought provoking read. *The Refractive Thinker Volume XI: Women in Leadership* covers topics that are so very important and relevant in today's society. Thank you for putting it out there and helping the women of today become even more successful women of tomorrow.

    Monica Skylling Mattson, *Mrs. Illinois-United States 2016, Confessions of an Aging Beauty Queen*

Leaders and those studying leadership will find this text worthwhile. While the traditional study of leadership places emphasis on gender roles, Dr. Glassman, and Dr. Lentz takes us into the 21st Century by suggesting that as we continue to operate globally, disconnecting gender from the leadership conversation is both evolutionary and necessary.

    Dr. Kimberly Rowland, *drrowlandplace.com*

THE REFRACTIVE THINKER®

AN ANTHOLOGY OF DOCTORAL WRITERS

VOLUME XI
Women in Leadership

Edited by Dr. Cheryl A. Lentz

THE REFRACTIVE THINKER® PRESS

The Refractive Thinker®: An Anthology of Higher Learning
Vol XI: Women in Leadership

The Refractive Thinker® Press
7124 Glyndon Trail NW
Albuquerque, NM 87114   USA

www.refractivethinker.com
blog: http://www.dissertationpublishing.com

All rights reserved. No part of this book may be reproduced or transmitted in any form or by any means, graphic, electronic or mechanical, including photocopying, recording, taping, Web distribution, or by any informational storage and retrieval system without written permission from the publisher except for the inclusion of brief quotations in a review or scholarly reference.

Books are available through The Refractive Thinker® Press at special discounts for bulk purchases for the purpose of sales promotion, seminar attendance, or educational purposes. Special volumes can be created for specific purposes and to organizational specifications. Please contact us for further details.

Individual authors own the copyright to their individual materials. The Refractive Thinker® Press has each author's permission to reprint.

 Please visit us on Facebook and like our Fan page. www.facebook.com/refractivethinker

Copyright © 2016 by The Refractive Thinker® Press
Managing Editor: Dr. Cheryl A. Lentz • DrCherylLentz@gmail.com

Library of Congress Control Number: 2013945437

Volume ISBNs   Soft Cover   978-0-9974399-0-8
               E-book/PDF   978-0-9974399-1-5
               *Kindle and electronic versions available

Refractive Thinker® logo by Joey Root; The Refractive Thinker® Press logo design by Jacqueline Teng; cover design and final production by Gary A. Rosenberg, www.thebookcouple.com.

Printed in the United States of America

10   9   8   7   6   5   4   3   2   1

Contents

Foreword, vii

Preface, ix

Acknowledgments, xi

CHAPTER 1
Refractive Mentoring Strategies for Rising Beyond Biases and Barriers to Leadership Promotions, 1
Dr. Gwendolyn C. Dooley

CHAPTER 2
Mentoring Women in Educational Leadership Through the Dissertation Process: A College Professor's Thoughts and Experiences, 17
Dr. Kathi H. Gibson

CHAPTER 3
Using Leadership to Improve Firm Performance Through Knowledge Management, 31
Dr. Cynthia J. Young

CHAPTER 4
Native American Women in Leadership Working Toward a Sustainable Future, 49
Dr. Janie Hall

CHAPTER 5
Creating Refractive Thinking in the Classroom to Inspire Accounting Leadership in Women, 61
Dr. Michelle L. Boese

CHAPTER 6

The Power of Promoting Women in Leadership Through Mentoring and Networking, 75

Dr. Patricia A. Champion & Dr. Linda J. Gutsch

CHAPTER 7

Women as Leaders, 95

Dr. Denise Mayo Moore

CHAPTER 8

Innovative Strategies for Women to Overcome Barriers in Pursuing Leadership Roles in Healthcare Organizations, 113

Dr. Jennifer Guerguis & Dr. Kirlos M. Guerguis

CHAPTER 9

A Story of Voice, 131

Dr. Laurie Maslak

CHAPTER 10

The Paradox of Color Coding Leadership: Pink for Girls and Blue for Boys? 153

Dr. Aaron Glassman & Dr. Cheryl A. Lentz

Index, 175

2016–2017 Catalog, 177

*You have to learn the rules of the game.
And then you have to play better than anyone else.*
—Albert Einstein

Foreword

Women leaders have made extraordinary progress in recent decades, both in terms of positional power and as influencers of the larger culture. Yes, women remain notably under-represented in certain sectors, but when contrasted with the centuries and millennia in which women's views and voices were almost entirely absent from the public sphere, the speed with which they have gained authority and begun making decisions at the highest levels is astonishing and of world-historical import.

The shift has occurred primarily because women themselves have spent the last 40 years or so working to carve and deepen cracks in glass ceilings of every kind. Organizations and institutions for the most part had to be pushed into getting on board, though over the last two decades many have instituted programs that support women's advancement. Both individual women's efforts and those of organizations have been aided by demographic, economic, and technological changes that have transformed how excellence in leadership is understood. More collaborative and inclusive models, which reflect the architecture of our dominant technologies and aspire to engage rather than command performance, have enabled women's best talents to flourish and be recognized and rewarded.

Throughout these decades, research has played a vital role in fostering women's leadership. In the early 1990s, researchers began documenting the distinctive nature of women's contributions, giving women confidence in the utility of acting on their best instincts and demonstrating to organizations the benefits of encouraging high potential women to pursue advancement. Later in the decade, research was instrumental in helping organizations recognize that simply hiring women in large numbers would not alone assure increased female representation at the top since women were rarely promoted at the same rate as men. While women's leadership had since the late 1980s been widely considered a *pipeline issue* that would solve itself as more women entered the workplace, the recognition that the pipeline was leaky led many organizations to consider how they might do a better job of retaining, engaging and developing talented women.

As the new century dawned, it became increasingly clear that achieving gender parity at the top would require a greater understanding of the more subtle challenges women face. Researchers in the academy, at think tanks such as Catalyst and notably at McKinsey in their highly influential Women Matter series, developed data that enabled women and organizations to gain more specific insights into what progress required. The key roles of organizational culture, differing expectations and benchmarks, underdeveloped internal and external networks, as well as the persistence of unconscious biases and assumptions, were all shown to play a role in hindering women's advancement and limiting their influence.

Mentoring and sponsorship programs, network building initiatives and career development intensives are among the fruits of this research, helping tens of thousands of women better position themselves as leaders. This back and forth traffic between research and deliverable programs has been a key factor in women's continuing progress, moving efforts beyond the realm of speculation and hope and rooting them in data.

This volume in the Refractive Thinker® series contains research gems that will influence how women's leadership is understood and supported in the years ahead. Fresh insights into mentoring and coaching practices, an examination of the importance of developing a voice, the impact of continued shifts in demographics, and the role of women in specific cultures in articulating a sustainable vision of the future: such contributions will expand and enrich the programmatic offerings that help speed women on their leadership journeys in the future.

And women's leadership matters not just because a healthy and economically vibrant society thrives on diversity and inclusion, but because the one-sided top down male model that prevailed in the industrial era cannot addresses the challenges of our hyper-connected global economy, in which the primary currency, the chief determinant of value, lies, as Peter Drucker presciently saw, not in capital goods but in human knowledge. The increasing movement of women into decision-making roles, and their ability to exercise influence at the highest levels, is what our global culture requires to move safely and prosperously forward.

—Sally Helgesen
Author of *The Female Vision, The Female Advantage, The Web of Inclusion,* and *Thriving in 24/7*

About the Author...

Sally Helgesen, the author of six books, has been delivering women's leadership programs for over 25 years. As a speaker and consultant, she has helped women in corporations, partnership firms, universities and associations around the world to gain a more powerful understanding of how to use their skills to maximum advantage.

Sally's most recent book, *The Female Vision: Women's Real Power at Work,* explores how women's strategic insights can strengthen their careers and benefit their organizations. Her best-selling *The Female Advantage: Women's Ways of Leadership,* hailed as *the classic work* on women's leadership styles, has been continuously in print since 1990 and translated into 12 languages. *The Web of Inclusion: A New Architecture for Building Great Organizations* was cited in The Wall Street Journal as one of the best books on leadership of all time and is credited with bringing the language of inclusion into business.

Clients include Chevron, Google, IBM, Eli Lilly, BHP Billiton Melbourne, Navigant, Leadership California, Morgan Stanley, Lincoln Financial Group, The World Bank, The West Point Military Academy, Boston Scientific, Orrick LLP, Roschier LLP Helsinki, ING Amsterdam, and The Distributed Education Network, Oslo.

Sally has consulted with UNDP on building more inclusive country offices in Africa and Asia, led seminars at the Harvard Graduate School of Education and Smith College, and been visiting scholar at Northwestern University, U-Nordic, Stockholm and the Lauriston Institute, Melbourne. She is a contributing editor and monthly columnist for Strategy + Business magazine and a member of The Learning Network and the International Women's Forum. She lives in Chatham NY.

Preface

Welcome to the award winning Refractive Thinker® Doctoral Anthology Series. We are thrilled to have you join us for the 13th volume in the series (Vol II was published 3 times), *Volume XI: Women in Leadership*. Join us as we continue to celebrate the accomplishments of doctoral scholars from around the globe.

Our mission continues to be to get research off the coffee table, out of the Ivory Tower, and into the hands of people who cannot only use, but also benefit from the many insights and wisdom found from research results. The goal is to continue to bridge the gap from the halls of academia into the halls of the business world. The Refractive Thinker® series continues to offer a resource by the many contributing doctoral scholars as they offer their chapter summaries of doctoral research that are well beyond the boundaries of a traditional textbook. Instead, the goal for this series is to use refractive thinking strategies to push the boundaries beyond conventional wisdom and to explore the paths not yet traveled.

As we move toward the Fall 2016 Presidential election within the United States, this peer-reviewed publication offers readers insights and solutions to various challenges regarding *Women in Leadership,* such as refractive mentoring strategies for rising beyond biases, mentoring women in educational leadership, using leadership to improve firm performance through knowledge management, Native American Women in leadership working toward a sustainable future, creating refractive thinking in the classroom to inspire accounting leadership in women, the power of promoting women in leadership through mentoring and networking, innovative strategies for women to overcome barriers in pursuing leadership roles in healthcare organizations, a story of voice, and the paradox of the color coding of leadership, asking the question if leadership comes in pink for girls and blue for boys. Our hope is that you will find answers regarding effective strategies regarding women in leadership to help guide your efforts in the boardroom, as well as the work space as part of this special edition *Women in Leadership* that have come from the research and pens of professional academicians and scholars around the world. The premise is to think not only *outside the box,* but also *beyond the box,* to create new solutions, to ask new questions, to proceed forward on new roads not yet explored or traveled. Our premise is to review academic research in a simple to digest executive summary format to offer new ways for business to think about effective practices for strategies in their business based on what new research has to offer.

With this volume, we add a new dimension to the series where Dr. Cheryl Lentz, *The Academic Entrepreneur* will conclude each chapter from a business point of view to link this doctoral research to applications for your business.

Remember, not only does *The Refractive Thinker*® series offer a physical book, we offer eBooks (Kindle, Nook, and Adobe eReader), and eChapters (individual chapters by author) that highlight the writings of your favorite Refractive Thinker® scholars, available through our website: http://www.RefractiveThinker.com, as well as www.Amazon.com . Be sure to also visit our Facebook page, Twitter, our YouTube Channel, and our groups on LinkedIN® for further discussions regarding the many ideas presented here.

We look forward to your continued support and interest of the more than 130 scholars within the Refractive Thinker® doctoral community who contributed to this multi award winning anthology series from around the globe. Our mission that began with Volume 1 many years ago is to bring research out of academia for application in the world of business to provide answers to the many questions asked.

Acknowledgments

The foundation of scholarly research embraces the art of asking questions—to validate and affirm, what we do, and why. Through asking the right questions, the right answers are found. Leaders often challenge the status quo, to offer alternatives and new directions, to dare to try something bold and audacious, to try something that has never been tried before. This 13th publication of our beloved award winning *Refractive Thinker®* series required the continued belief in this new publishing model, of a peer-reviewed doctoral anthology, by those willing to continue forward on this voyage.

As a result, let me express my gratitude for the help of many who made this collaboration possible. First, let me offer a special thank you to our Peer Review Board, to include Dr. Judy Fisher-Blando, Dr. Ron Jones, Dr. Elmer Hall, and myself; and our Board of Advisors to include: Brian Jud, Dr. Jody Sandwisch, Kevin Dunn, Dr. Tammi Reilly, and myself.

My gratitude extends with a well-deserved thank you to our production team: Gary Rosenberg (production specialist) and Joey Root, designer of the Refractive Thinker® logo.

—Dr. Cheryl Lentz

Refractive Mentoring Strategies for Rising Beyond Biases and Barriers to Leadership Promotions

Dr. Gwendolyn C. Dooley

Women adopt various traditional titles for multiple roles such as mother, aunt, grandmother, professional, coach, friend, and wife. Other nontraditional titles are *super-mom, super-woman, and super-professional*, which suggests the ability to complete various tasks simultaneously and efficiently. Women, as refractive thinkers, use the same *out of the box* thinking in the superwoman roles, although overcoming workplace barriers and biases appear unachievable when seeking promotion to administrative and executive positions. Research data regarding the number of senior executives or administrators working in all business, government, and industrial organizations show a consistent underrepresentation of women and minorities (McDonald & Westphal, 2013). Only 17.8% of law partners are women (Cody, 2105). Although Cody's (2015) data singularly focused on women lawyers, a goal for most career women is to earn a senior management position in corporate, education, government, professional, and industrial organizations (Kaul &Mathur, 2012). The appearance of gender biases or barriers for women is not fully known because research data appear to focus on male to female biases (a singular focus) rather than the multiplicity of gender and generational factors present in the workforce. Traditional mentoring programs appear to be a *cookie cutter* approach for a male leadership workplace rather than an innovative model that provide women the flexibility to become administrators while balancing the needs of family and other social activities. The chapter is a review of literature on the underrepresentation of women leaders in junior and senior positions. The purpose of this chapter is to discuss the need for institutional mentoring programs that includes refractive thinking strategies to address barriers of gender bias and the lack of sustainable mentoring opportunities design for women seeking executive and administrative positions.

Background of the Problem

What is not known is whether persistent administrative and executive underrepresentation for women and minorities link to a lack of motivation and experience, generational differences, ethnicity, same gender partiality, or self-preservation. Limited research exists concerning gender bias or the lack of mentoring experiences from the perspectives of women aspiring to become junior or senior leaders. Little to no research concerning innovative strategies *or out of the box thinking* to overcome challenges for women promotion to administrative positions exist. According to Ibarra, Ely, and Kolb (2013), limited access to administrative and executive positions is a disruption of a learning cycle within organizations. Research concerning refractive thinking to reduce barriers to administrative positions could increase women promotion opportunities. Based on the recommendation of McDonald and Westphal (2013), a discussion concerning the underrepresentation of women and minorities in major organizations is presented in this review of literature. Perhaps a sustainability plan for talented and hard working women could improve the low underrepresentation of women leaders.

Problem

According to McDonald and Westphal (2013) and Mathur (2012), a substantial underrepresentation of women and racial minorities exists in corporate senior leadership positions, supporting further study because of a negative societal effect. Although women diversity appears to be *trending* in the research literature for male to female (or vice versa) groups, innovative approaches to reduce gender bias appear to be unexplored for same genders, genders from different generations, or transgenders. Kaul and Mathur (2012) shared that 28% of women receive a low wage within global production chains, which show a bias for earnings between male and female groups. Hill (2013) reported that both women and men employment growth remained constant with a minimal increase during 2007 recession. Despite these percentages, the underrepresentation of women in junior and leadership positions show minimal change.

Recent data, concerning gender gaps, focus on the glass ceiling (Murray & Syed, 2010), diversity (McDonald & Westphal, 2013), gender pay (Rubery, Grimshaw, & Figueiredo, 2005), and job satisfaction (Gabriel & Schmitz, 2007), rather than specific experiences of bias indifferences among women in work environments. The purpose of this qualitative, exploratory research is to explore findings on personal and professional biases that prevent upward mobility for women and also sustainable mentoring opportunities in the work environment design to improve promotion for women to administrative roles. The problem explored is if persistent underrepresentation of women links to a lack of motivation and experience, generational differences, ethnicity, same gender partiality, or self-preservation. Exploring this problem may cause honest discourse about gender inequities and may cause executive leaders to plan and implement sustainable mentoring programs targeting women aspiring for senior leadership positions.

Research Questions

A plethora of research exists concerning workplace gender diversity, performance, and ethnic differences, but not about other factors such as generational differences, ethnicity, same gender partiality, or self-preservation (Kaul & Mathur, 2012; Leslie, Snyder, & Glomb, 2013). Also, Leslie et al. (2013) indicated there are limited findings regarding workplace disparities among ethnic groups (Asian, Black, Hispanic, and Native American). For the purpose of this qualitative exploration, the goal is to explore literature to determine a need for further research on the following questions.

1. Is there persistent underrepresentation of women in administrative and executive positions in all occupational industries in the 21st century?

2. Is the persistent underrepresentation of women because of organizational culture?

3. Does persistent underrepresentation of women link to a lack of motivation and experience, generational differences, ethnicity, same gender partiality, or self-preservation?

4. What is the effect of mentoring programs on gender biases, stereotyping, organizational culture, and upward mobility for women in the 21st century?

5. What are the implications of implementing systemic mentoring programs regardless of gender, ethnicity, or sexual orientation?

6. How would refractive thinking strategies impact perceived barriers to administrative promotion?

When studying issues of gender bias within a leader perspective or organizational context, a researcher must determine if organizational culture, is a primary focus of study, rather than leader bias

(Mills, 2002). A researcher must determine whether a one-time view of the issues is adequate to capture actual occurrences of biased acts rather than a longer data collection period (Mills, 2002). Because this chapter is a qualitative literature exploration, a determination of a qualitative methodological data collection procedure will occur. But, a recommendation is to consider either a case study or phenomenological research design to address lived experiences or to specifically study cultural contexts to gain current, in-depth knowledge of systemic gender biases or barriers to administrative or executive positions.

Conceptual Framework

Building on the work of Murray and Syed (2010), the intent is to expand the idea that organizational cultures and traditions could be primary factors for the persistent underrepresentation experienced by women desiring junior and senior leadership positions as proclaimed by McDonald and Westphal (2013). Murray and Syed focused on the term *gendering or gendered lenses* meaning the "common world views . . . [that are] fixed . . . understood [and] . . . influence[d] social patterns of behaviour within organisations and wider society" (p. 277). The definition of gendering by Murray and Syed appeared to expand the definition provided by Sharpe and Bradley (1998) who also defined the term as a "fixed attributes of women and men . . . a social process . . . [and] concerned with how understandings of sexual difference shape institutions, practices, and relationships" (p. 1). Based on these definitions, there appears to be an institutional culture of gender biases supported by varying contexts such as personnel practices, processes, and societal values. These contextual factors require study beyond common women and men differences, discrimination, and pay gaps, but actual cultural and habitual practices that foster incessant gender bias.

The study of gendering requires an in-depth exploration or examination of how gender bias is culturally and perhaps socially entrenched in operational practices by leaders and followers, which requires capturing lived systemic experiences of women who perceive differences and barriers to promotion beyond feministic and masculinity perceptions (Sharpe & Bradley, 1998). However, Lanaj and Hollenbeck (2015) suggested that gender role theory (authored by Eagly, 1987) is a foundational framework when exploring "gender-specific societal role and behavioral expectations" (p. 1477). Gendering and gender role theory appear to overlap, and could be co-operational frameworks for future research if exploring systemic mentoring program impact on gender bias and promotional opportunities for leadership development and effectiveness; creating a paradigm shift concerning unilateral acceptance regardless of gender, ethnicities, or sexuality.

Murray and Syed (2010) reported lived experiences and observations of women in legal and institutional contexts focusing on equal employment opportunity, organizational policies and procedures, and workplace cultures as an approach to discovery of specific factors causing barriers. Although the focus of gendering is within the scope of the problem explored in this chapter, workplace cultures, leader practices, individual refractive thinking practices, and personal biases are additional factors requiring exploration. The scope of gendering is the framework for this chapter to address the scope of the problem.

Gender Bias

Researchers noted numerous biases in the workforce for women. According to Evans (2011), out of 12 board members, 15.4% of women have corporate officer positions, 14.8% are board members, and 2.4% are chief executives in Fortune 500 organizations. Evans noted that gender stereotype was a primary barrier for women promotion to senior level administrative positions. Additional barriers noted by Evans were stereotypical to women needing flexible work schedules that often lead to exclusion from communicative or social networks, lack of positive mentors, and no sustainability strategies. Singh (2003) suggested gender considerations are a conscious and unconscious act during work transactions. Ten years later, Ibarra et al. (2013) confirmed a continuing phenomenon in the 21st century of an unawareness by women experiencing gender bias, specifically between same genders (male to male or female to female). Perhaps exploring same gender bias is an additional research question for qualitative and quantitative research.

Traditions

Apparently, more men garner leadership roles than women do. Evans (2011) noted that women are "atypical leaders" [while men are] "default leaders" (p. 62), which support societal and cultural traditions. Lanaj and Hollenbeck (2015) identified distinct qualities concerning the attributes of men (agentic: assertiveness, confidence, and independence) compared to women (communal: helpfulness, nurturance, kindness). Men often strive to obtain a dominate leadership or managerial role, while women pursue follower positions (Singh, 2003). Perhaps women are comfortable in follower roles for these reasons:

1. Women are nurturers and often avoid conflicts to foster a harmonic workplace,

2. Women may find it difficult to oppose unsupportive leaders who are *gatekeepers* to junior or senior level positions, and

3. Some women, particularly single mothers, become less dominate because of a need to meet economic family obligations.

Second Generation Gender Bias

Lake, Harvey, and Bosco (2014) suggested that 15% of women reported directly experiencing gender bias and 13% perceived a denial of an increase in pay. When women register concerns about these inequities, biased rhetoric occurs from male counterparts and cause inaction defining *second-generation gender bias*. Ibarra et al. (2013) suggested that *second generation gender bias* is ethical generational perceptions such as culture (personal and organizational), practices, connections, and educational aptitudes (Bhatia & Amati, 2010). Lake et al. suggested that *second generation gender bias* supports the misconception that gender bias no longer exists in the workplace.

Is There Generational Bias?

Most people would claim yes because of the four generations working together with varying work and personal values. According to Schullery (2013), the workplace includes four generational work groups: (a) "Silent Generation, also known as Traditionalists (1925–1945), (b) Baby Boomers (1946–1964), (c) Generation X or GenX (1965–1981), and (d) the Millennials (1982–1999), known as Net Gen, Gen Y, GenerationMe, Gen Net, and Digital Natives" (p. 253). Further, Hill (2013) reported that 55% of workers (ages 60 to 64) employed in 2010, which documents an increase from 2000 of 47% among ages 50s, 60s or 70s, remains employed beyond designated years of service. However, part of the possible slow progress of women (and younger generations) receiving opportunities for promotion is the delayed retirement of the older workforce. The delay of older workers retiring indicates a contributing factor for younger generations receiving little to no access to leadership positions as well and a possible contributing factor of generational bias. Leaders gain a workforce with longevity and validated experiences and knowledge when older workers remain in the workforce longer. The delay in retirement denies promotable opportunities for younger women and other generations vying for leadership roles. A lack of succession planning to retain specific operational knowledge of older workers / leaders creates gaps and limit continuity. Perhaps succession (mentoring) programs could be an added research question for further research.

Inconsistent findings concerning generational differences and values regarding women promotion to administrative position appears in the literature. An "absence of a unifying theory, the lack of a clear pattern of findings, and the conceptual ambiguity about generational membership" was noted by Cox and Coulton (2015, p. 372), justifying a need for further research. Lyons, Urick, Kuron, and Schweitzer (2015) indicated limited data exist to support differences in work outcome as well as Brink, Zondag, and Crenshaw (2015) and Cox and Coulton. Expanding the conversation on stereotype, Brink et al. and Cox and Coulton noted a commonality of issues among all generational groups. A few biases include perceptions that Baby Boomers have work stresses and appear materialistic, while Millennials value technological advances, but may be perceived cynical (Cox & Coulton, 2015) to older work groups. Biased barriers, another inconsistent finding, are because of unrecognizable differences in the varying values of multiple generational group members (Schullery, 2013). Another inconsistent finding includes the differing attitudes and behaviors because of biases and preferences among a multigenerational work environment (Yi & Yisheng, 2015). Because of inconsistent findings concerning unifying theory and patterns of findings, further research could support further study.

Addressing Gender Barriers Through Mentoring

Bhatia and Amati (2010) suggested that formal and informal programs are primary strategies for addressing gender bias in academic and professional settings. Cody (2015) reported success by increasing the number of women in mentoring programs using an innovative approach to recruiting a pre-planned number of women. According to Cody, women are automatically selecting the accounting occupation because some firms offer specific benefits such as honoring work-life commitments. Based on leader practices at the accounting firm, women more aggressive because work options include traditional and flexible hours. Collins, Lewis, Stracke, and Vanderheide (2014) also suggested that diverse work strategies that women use to have successful career paths. Collins et al. promoted success factors of mentoring programs as opportunities for exploration for career paths across academic disciplines. However, there was no link to other career pathways. Other success factors of systemic mentoring programs are engagement, career success (Zachary, 2015), and gender diversity (An Alliance for Women, 2015).

Conclusion

The Alliance for Women (2015) recommended diversity as a *right now* priority and . . . "when gender diversity is achieved, our work is done" (p. 8). Most woman affected by gender bias and are denied opportunities for promotion may agree with the priority statement and may also share in an open discussion concerning barriers to promotion. Although generational differences, the literature did not show if bias or barriers were specifically occurring from one generation to another. Specifically, male to female biases appear in research findings rather than issues among generations and same gender regarding promotion to administrative and executive positions. Innovative mentoring practices appeared to enable women to enter into leadership roles. However, only one program that specifically targeted women was located in the review of the literature. The program identified by Cody (2015) is innovative because the leaders of the accounting firm recognized the conflicting obligations that women have that could prevent continuity in the workplace. Because the firm leaders used innovative mentoring and coaching practices, a refractive thinking approach, workplace bias decreased, and confidence levels increased leading to increased productivity levels (Cody, 2015). Absent from the literature were discussions by women concerning mentoring needs and how open conversations concerning workplace bias could be beneficial for improving promotion opportunities for women leaders. Systemic mentoring plans using refractive thinking principles could provide a remedy for misconceived notions that women desiring to balance the needs of the family would not be comparable to the talents of men without similar responsibilities in the home. Absent from the literature is data on same gender and generational biases. Exploration concerning biases experienced by same gender and generational groups provides opportunities for open discourse using refractive thinking principles to address communication and promotion barriers.

THOUGHTS FROM THE ACADEMIC ENTREPRENEUR

The problem to be solved:

- If persistent underrepresentation of women links to a lack of motivation and experience, generational differences, ethnicity, same gender partiality, or self-preservation.

The goals:

- Explore literature to determine a need for further research on barriers to promotion, gender biases, and generational differences.

- Explore innovative mentoring practices designed to increase women representation to administrative and executive positions.

The questions to ask:

- Is there persistent underrepresentation of women in administrative and executive positions in all occupational industries in the 21st century?
- Is the persistent underrepresentation of women because of organizational culture?
- Does persistent underrepresentation of women link to a lack of motivation and experience, generational differences, ethnicity, same gender partiality, or self-preservation?
- What is the effect of mentoring programs on gender biases, stereotyping, organizational culture, and upward mobility for women in the 21st century?
- What are the implications of implementing systemic mentoring programs regardless of gender, ethnicity, or sexual orientation?
- How would refractive thinking strategies impact perceived barriers to administrative promotion?

Today's Business Application:

- Understanding innovative mentoring practices and programs that may reduce perceived biases and barriers for women seeking administrative positions.
- Empowering women to prepare for leadership roles by participating in mentoring programs.
- Empowering leaders with research data on the importance of intentional mentoring programs for women.

REFERENCES

An Alliance for Women. (2015). *New Zealand Management, 64*(5), 8. Retrieved from https://www.highbeam.com/doc/1G1-427423049.html

Barton, D., Devillard, S., & Hazlewood, J. (2015). Gender equality: Taking stock of where we are. *McKinsey Quarterly,* (4), 86–89. Retrieved from http://www.mckinsey.com/business-functions/organization/our-insights/gender-equality-taking-stock-of-where-we-are

Bhatia, S., & Amati, J. P. (2010). 'If these women can do it, I can do it, too': Building women engineering leaders through graduate peer mentoring. *Leadership & Management in Engineering, 10*(4), 174–184. doi:10.1061/(ASCE)LM.1943-5630.0000081

Brink, K. E., Zondag, M. M., & Crenshaw, J. L. (2015). Generation is a culture construct. *Industrial & Organizational Psychology, 8,* 335–340. doi:10.1017/iop.2015.45

Cody, T. (2015). Breaking barriers. *Accounting Today, 29*(4), 8–9. Retrieved from http://www.accountingtoday.com/news/firm-profession/practice-profile-breaking-barriers-74156-1.html

Collins, A., Lewis, I., Stracke, E., & Vanderheide, R. (2014). Talking career across disciplines: Peer group mentoring for women academics. *International Journal of Evidence Based Coaching & Mentoring, 12*(1), 92–108. Retrieved from http://ijebcm.brookes.ac.uk/documents/vol12issue1-paper-07.pdf

Cox, C. B., & Coulton, G. (2015). Fire all the boomers: How generational labeling legitimizes age discrimination. *Industrial & Organizational Psychology, 8,* 372–376. doi:10.1017/iop.2015.52

Evans, D. (2011). Room at the top: Advancement and equity for women in the business world. *National Civic Review, 100*(2), 62–64. doi:10.1002/ncr.20061

Gabriel, P. E. & Schmitz, S. (2007, June). Gender differences among women: Gender differences in occupational distributions among workers. *Monthly Labor Review.* Retrieved from http://www.bls.gov/opub/mlr/2007/06/art2full.pdf

Hill, K. L. (2013). We've come a long way, baby, or have we? *Journal of Organizational Culture, Communications & Conflict, 17*(2), 29–36. Retrieved from https://www.highbeam.com/doc/1P3-3148305221.html

Ibarra, H., Ely, R., & Kolb, D. (2013). Women rising: The unseen barriers (cover story). *Harvard Business Review, 91*(9), 60–67. Retrieved from https://hbr.org/2013/09/women-rising-the-unseen-barriers/ar/1

Kidder, D. L., & Parks, J. M. (2001). The good soldier: who is s(he)? *Journal of Organizational Behavior, 22,* 939–959. doi:10.1002/job.119

Lanaj, K., & Hollenbeck, J. R. (2015). Leadership over emergence in self-managing teams: The role of gender and countervailing biases. *Academy of Management Journal, 58,* 1476–1494. doi:10.5465/amj.2013.0303

Lake, D., Harvey, D., & Bosco, S. (2014). Second generation gender bias: An invisible issue. *Proceedings for the Northeast Region Decision Sciences Institute (NEDSI)*, 1122–1128.

Leslie, L. M., Snyder, M., & Glomb, T. M. (2013). Who gives?: Multilevel effects of gender and ethnicity on workplace charitable giving. *Journal of Applied Psychology, 98*(1), 49–62. doi:10.1037/a0029943

Lyons, S., Urick, M., Kuron, L., & Schweitzer, L. (2015). Generational differences in the workplace: There is complexity beyond the stereotypes. *Industrial & Organizational Psychology, 8*, 346–356. doi:10.1017/iop.2015.48

Mathur, A. N. (2012). New paradigms for gender inclusivity: Theory and best practices. *Vikalpa: The Journal for Decision Makers, 37*(3), 155–157.

McDonald. M. L., & Westphal, J. D. (2013). Access denied: Low mentoring of women and minority first time directors and its negative effects on appointments to additional boards. *Academy of Management Journal, 56*, 1169–1198. doi:10.5465/amj.2011.0230

Mills, A. J. (2002). Studying the gendering of organizational culture over time: Concerns, issues, and strategies. *Gender, Work & Organization, 9*(3), 286. doi:10.1111/1468-0432.00161

Murray, P. A., & Syed, J. (2010). Gendered observations and experiences in executive women's work. *Human Resource Management Journal, 20*(3), 277–293. doi:10.1111/j.1748-8583.2009.00113.x

Rubery, J., Grimshaw, D., & Figueiredo, H. (2005). How to close the gender pay gap in Europe: Towards the gender mainstreaming of pay policy. *Industrial Relations Journal, 36*(3), 184–213. doi:10.1111/j.1468-2338.2005.00353.x

Schullery, N. M. (2013). Workplace engagement and generational differences in values. *Business Communication Quarterly, 76*(2), 252–265. doi:10.1177/1080569913476543

Singh, K. (2003). Women managers: Perception vs performance analysis. *Journal of Management Research (09725814), 3*(1), 31–42. Retrieved from http://connection.ebscohost.com/c/articles/9867968/women-managers

Sharpe, P., & Bradley, H. (1998, Spring). Gendering work: Historical approaches. *Labour History Review (Maney Publishing)*, 1–3. Retrieved from http://connection.ebscohost.com/c/editorials/4049820/gendering-work-historical-approaches

Smith, R. A. (2002). Race, gender, and authority in the workplace: Theory and research. *Annual Review of Sociology, 28*, 509–542. doi:10.1146/annurev.soc.28.110601.141048

Yi, W., & Yisheng, P. (2015). An alternative approach to understanding generational differences. *Industrial & Organizational Psychology, 8*, 390–395. doi:10.1017/iop.2015.56

Zachary, L. J. (2015). Seven success strategies for mentoring program managers. *TD: Talent Development, 69*(2), 76–77. Retrieved from http://www.centerformentoringexcellence.com/wp-content/uploads/2015/02/Zachary.pdf

About the Author...

Dr. Gwendolyn C. Dooley, a native of Brooksville, MS, but currently resides in Jackson, MS. Gwen completed high school at Noxubee County High School in Macon, MS; and a Bachelor of Science Degree in Office Administration and Master of Public Policy and Administration Degree at Jackson State University in Jackson, MS. The Doctorate in Organizational Leaderships was completed at Nova Southeastern University in Ft. Lauderdale, Florida. She is currently completing a second Doctorate in Business Administration at Walden University in Minneapolis, MN.

Dr. Gwen is an adjunct faculty for institutions for higher learning (Walden University, Grand Canyon University, and the University of Phoenix). More than 27 years of work experience include working at Jackson State University and Alcorn State University as the Director of Academic Programs and the Assistant Director for Honors College, respectively. Currently, Dr. Dooley works with doctoral students in completing degree programs in business administration and education. She is a member of the Mortar Board National College Senior Honor Society and the Golden Key International Honour Society.

For consulting, doctoral coaching, and editing, please email: assessmentedsolutions@gmail.com

2

Mentoring Women in Educational Leadership through the Dissertation Process: A College Professor's Thoughts and Experiences

Dr. Kathi H. Gibson

The efforts toward school reform, the latest educational craze, and even the whimsical political platforms of this era challenge women in educational leadership roles. Yet the expectation from stakeholders is for leaders to elevate students to their zenith of academic productivity, regardless of background or socioeconomic status. A twenty-first -century aphorism in educational arenas is *the lead learner*. Fullan (2014) defined the lead learner as one who models learning and essentially shapes the conditions whereby continuous learning occurs within an organization. Becoming the lead learner is conceptually positive and may move the leader steps closer to self-actualization, or a state of full intellectual potential (Cohen, 2011). Toward becoming a lead learner, some school leaders embark on the journey of acquiring a doctorate degree. Yet, far too many candidates finish the coursework, and end up *All But Dissertation* (ABD). Educational research and national data report that the doctoral completion rate is approximately 50% (Butin, 2010; Council of Graduate Schools Ph.D Completion Project, 2008).

The cooperative learning spirit within many graduate classes often facilitates completion of the doctoral coursework. Graduate students typically begin a doctoral program in cohorts. Students bond and establish esprit de corps. Face-to-face learning modules and ongoing communication between students and instructors help instill a *stick-to-it-iveness* that propels the students through the coursework. Upon completion of the coursework, doctoral students disperse to their individual milieus, and some lose touch with cohort members and instructors. Students who enjoyed the benefits of communicating and collaborating with cohort members find themselves loners with an astronomical undertaking: writing the dissertation. This transition to independent scholar is often difficult for students (Gardner, 2008).

In the words of some researchers, navigating a doctoral program to completion can be a daunting task (Holmes, Danner, Gibson, & Woods, 2016). Foss and Waters (2007) speculated that completing the dissertation process entails 29 steps and 1,078 hours. Research showed that women can take longer to complete their doctorate for varying reasons (Maher, Ford, & Thompson, 2004). Holmes et al. (2016) reported from a study conducted by Bair and Haworth (1999) that the dissertation process is a common cause of attrition among doctoral students.

During the dissertation writing process, the advisor or the dissertation chair may be the only bond that a student has to the college and academia. Doctoral faculty mean well and make genuine attempts to facilitate the process, but they remain busy teaching classes, performing their own research, and conducting other university services (Foss & Waters, 2007), leaving students to their own means. According to Tinto (2006), "While most faculty are willing to publicly proclaim the importance of retaining each and every student, they typically do not see retaining students as their job" (p. 9). Some faculty might argue the acceptability of this hands-off approach to student retention, whereas others might suggest the contrary. Putsche, Storrs, Lewis, and Haylett (2008) found the following benefits of students having a mentor:

"increased retention, lower drop-out rates, improved academic performance, greater access to academic resources for students, improved post graduate opportunities, and improved personal satisfaction" (p. 514). Thus, acquiring an academic mentor may be the difference between a student becoming stymied in the process or completing the dissertation.

Mentors can support mentees and show them the ropes (Bloom, Castagna, Moir, & Warren, 2005). Neblett (2004) believed "a mentor can inspire someone to push beyond his or her own perceived limitations. . ." (p. 6). Crawford (2010) defined a mentor as one with expertise who teachers, counsels, inspires, and develops the abilities and knowledge of others. An academic mentor is one with a proven record of research, teaching, and academic leadership (University College Dublin, 2016). Revis-Pyke (2010) paraphrased Pride (2005) and Wallace (2000) when asserting that mentoring entails an important relationship between the student and the academic advisor; this relationship can seriously affect the student's success. Good mentors are trustworthy, caring, and committed, and a good mentor–mentee relationship begins with establishing comfort with each other, as well as good communication (Gardiner, Enomoto, & Grogan, 2000).

In 2011, a U.S. Department of Education grant received by a small university in the South sought to build leadership capacity in select, low-wealth school districts by implementing district-wide professional learning communities. To implement the grant's goals, the university hired five mentors, all retired principals or superintendents. Prior to working with the school leaders, the mentors received extensive training on research-based mentoring practices. The mentors visited the mentees several times monthly to support the district-wide initiative. Regular phone calls and e-mails helped facilitate positive mentor–mentee relationships and communication. This 5-year appointment proved to be a priceless venture, and the residual effects positioned me for the work ahead as an academic mentor. Moreover, I acquired a myriad of mentoring experiences, as well as strong relational skills.

Through the grant, I learned that mentoring school leaders (i.e., female leaders) entails being flexible, serving as a confidant, developing a *whatever-it-takes-to-be-successful* disposition, and possessing the capacity to build positive relationships. Academic mentors need many of the same skills in conjunction with an array of technical skills unique to dissertation writing. In addition, many doctoral candidates need support in the theoretical thinking and technical writing aspects required in the dissertation writing process. Women may mask their deficiencies because they prefer hiding them from the mentor. Thus, good relationships are fundamental. In a study that analyzed factors that constrain, facilitate, or differentiate degree progress, Maher et al. (2004) found that doctoral students who finish their programs early most often establish and maintain a positive working relationship with faculty members or their major advisor.

True mentors understand the need to build relationships first. Once accomplished, the mentor is a confidant, listening ear, and invaluable facilitator of the process. The mentor must be sensitive to the "multiplicity of women" (Gardiner et al., 2000, p. 109) and know how to ask questions that will cause the mentee to articulate personal and academic needs. Challenges unique to women such as "unequal benchmarks for success" (Gardiner et al., 2000, p. 109) or problems balancing work, family, and dissertation writing may interrupt the scholar's progress. Gardiner et al. (2000) observed that "good mentors connect well on an emotional and personal level with their protégés" (p. 53). Empathic listening improves understanding and helps build trust and respect (Salem, 2003).

A search of the literature revealed limited research on mentoring or mentoring female doctoral students. Further literature searches showed even fewer studies on mentoring women in educational leadership through the dissertation process, thus substantiating the importance of capturing data from the lived experiences of the subject in this study, hereafter referred to as Subject A. Understanding how Subject A described the mentor–mentee relationship with her female faculty academic mentor during the dissertation writing process is important to this body of research. In qualitative research, the researcher selects people or the person who can best help the researcher understand the central phenomenon. Moreover, the researcher may study a single individual (Creswell, 2012).

Subject A is an African American female principal. She is an experienced educator of 19 years and served as a school administrator for 14 of those 19 years. As part of the implementation of the U.S. Department of Education grant described earlier, I mentored Subject A. When I became acquainted with Subject A, I had been in a mentor–mentee relationship with the former principal who served prior to Subject A. Upon his retirement, I remained the principal mentor, but worked with Subject A. Ironically, Subject A was ABD and a student attending the university where I taught. (Note: The university mentioned above is not the same university that received and implemented the U.S. Department of Education grant).

Subject A approached the dean of the university and requested that I serve as the new chair of her dissertation committee. Upon the dean granting her request, I became her academic mentor. By synthesizing formal mentoring skills and the academic mentoring skills described earlier, I helped move the dissertation writing process along. After a little more than 2 years, the student defended her dissertation and graduated.

Revis-Pyke (2010) completed a dissertation titled *Benefits of Mentoring Female Doctoral Students: Outcomes of Dissertation Centric Interactions with Female Faculty Academic Mentors*. The purpose of the study was "to explore how female doctoral students describe their relationship with their female faculty academic mentor during the dissertation process" (Revis-Pyke, 2010, p. 1). A purposeful sample of 12 female doctoral students (nine Caucasians, two African Americans, and one person of multiple ethnicities) engaged in the process of writing their dissertation participated in the study by completing a web-based questionnaire. The following questions guided the data collection process:

1. Have you created any type of personal or networking groups while writing your dissertation?

2. What characteristics of your female faculty academic mentor do you value?

3. Do you believe your relationship with your faculty academic mentor has improved your performance in the dissertation writing process?

4. Describe your relationship with the faculty academic mentor?

5. Do you believe your relationship with your faculty academic mentor has enriched your learning experience as a doctoral student?

6. Were there times in your dissertation writing process that you considered leaving the program? To transfer to another university? To leave the program entirely? (Revis-Pyke, 2010)

The researcher grouped the data collected from the questionnaire into meaningful units. The researcher used the units to construct explanations, findings, and conclusions. Along with bracketed subthemes, five major themes emerged:

1. Support groups [graduate students / classmates, family, external support]

2. Positive attributes [accessible, encouraging, interested, honest]

3. Knowledge and experiences [expert, experienced, scholarly]

4. Relationships [collegial, adversarial, unequal]

5. Barriers and obstacles [time, minimal support, lack of experience and knowledge on the part of female faculty, academic mentor, faculty turnover]. (Revis-Pyke, 2010, p. 45)

    A definitive way that many mentors can assess their effectiveness is by getting input from their mentees (University of Washington, 2015). For me to understand how Subject A described the mentor–mentee relationship during the dissertation writing process, Subject A answered six of the same questions used in Revis-Pyke's (2010) research. The responses served as data for answering the central research question. An analysis of the major themes and the subthemes, as well as overlapping themes, and the number of times the participant mentioned the major or minor themes in her responses established the procedures used for assigning meaning to the data obtained from Subject A (Creswell, 2012).

Findings

Question 1: When asked, what characteristics of your female faculty academic mentor do you value positively, Subject A listed the following: dedication, commitment, sense of comfort, openness, good listener, effective communicator, and honesty.

Question 2: Subject A responded *yes* when asked, do you believe your relationship with your faculty academic mentor improved your performance in the dissertation writing process? The participant further stated, "My academic mentor would not accept less than professional writing and she modeled the expectations."

Question 3: When asked to describe the relationship with the faculty academic mentor, Student A offered the following descriptors: respectful, trustworthy, cooperative, caring, and genuine interest in my well-being.

Question 4: In response to the question, do you believe your relationship with your faculty academic mentor enriched your learning experience as a doctoral student, the participant answered, "Yes, I believe my relationship with my academic mentor enriched my learning experience as a doctoral student to a high level. If I did not have the aforementioned relationship with my faculty academic mentor, I would have given up."

Question 5: When asked whether there were times in your dissertation writing process that you considered leaving the program, to transfer to another university or to leave the program entirely, Subject A responded, "Yes, as I mentioned in the previous question . . . if it were not for my faculty academic mentor and our relationship, I would have transferred to another university to attempt to finish my dissertation or just left the program entirely. I had two previous faculty academic mentors who did not seem committed to me and my professional accomplishments."

Question 6: Subject A was asked, have you found any characteristic of your faculty academic mentor to be problematic? If so, describe. The participant answered, "Absolutely NOT!"

Conclusion and Recommendations

The objective of this qualitative study was to understand how Subject A described the mentor–mentee relationship with her female faculty academic mentor during the dissertation writing process. Subject A answered six of the questions used in an earlier qualitative research study by Revis-Pyke (2010). An analysis of the qualitative data indicated that Subject A described the relationship with her female faculty academic mentor as positive and credited the relationship for propelling her through the dissertation writing process. In response to question 1, the respondent listed the following valued characteristics of the female academic mentor:

dedication, commitment, sense of comfort, openness, good listener, effective communicator, and honesty. The data obtained from questions 2–6 revealed how Subject A described the mentor-mentee relationship, emphasizing the importance of the mentor-mentee relationship during the dissertation writing process. Positive relationships became a recurring theme in this study. The participant credited the positive relationship with her female faculty academic mentor for her improved performance in the dissertation writing process because her mentor forbade anything less than professional writing, as well as for her completion of the program rather than transferring or giving up. Peters (2003) believed that a supportive relationship enables the mentee to move to independence. Subject A described her relationship with her female faculty academic mentor using the following adjectives: respectful, trustworthy, cooperative, and caring. Gardiner et al. (2000) believed that good mentors are, specifically, trustworthy and caring. Essential elements of a mentoring relationship are respect, trust, and communication (U.S. Army, n.d.). Subject A concluded that the mentor showed a genuine interest in her well-being. Finally, when asked whether the mentor had problematic characteristics, Subject A stated, "Absolutely NOT."

The 50% attrition rate described by Butin (2010) and the Council of Graduate Schools PhD Completion Project (2008) substantiates the need to provide effective levels of support to doctoral students. Although this study does not purport to have definitive answers for reducing the attrition rate of female doctoral students in the field of educational leadership who are ABD, the findings certainly raise questions and ignite conversations for future research. Some scholars may expect a percentage of doctoral candidates to remain ABD. Other scholars may consider the 50% attrition rate unacceptable. Nonetheless, the findings of this study have highlighted the likely benefits [to females in leadership] of acquiring an academic mentor when navigating through the dissertation writing process. The results of this study may serve as a catalyst to raise awareness of the need for additional training for doctoral advisors and dissertation chairs.

Maher et al. (2004) stated the following:

> If higher education is to realize the benefits of the growing number of women doctoral students and potential women doctoral degree recipients, it must create an environment that supports them in their struggles and provides opportunities and resourceful strategies to meet the challenges posed by their worthy pursuit. (p. 403)

Whereas there is limited feasibility in making general statements based on this small sample, this study indicated the need for future research. Moreover, this researcher is vested in continuing research on mentoring women in leadership, especially as they progress through the dissertation writing progress. Finally, this researcher acknowledges that the future of her research is poised to provide higher education practitioners with alternative thinking necessary for the survival of female doctoral students in the 21st century.

THOUGHTS FROM THE ACADEMIC ENTREPRENEUR

The problem to be solved:
- Ineffective levels of support from higher education for women in leadership roles trying to navigate the dissertation writing process.

The goals:
- Understanding how women in leadership describe their academic mentor-mentee relationship during the dissertation writing process.

- Understanding if the academic mentor-mentee relationship can be fundamental to helping some women in educational leadership roles complete the dissertation writing process.

The questions to ask:
- How would you describe your relationship with your academic mentor-during the dissertation writing process?
- What characteristics of your female faculty academic mentor do you value?
- Do you believe your relationship with your faculty academic mentor improved your performance in the dissertation writing process?
- Do you believe your relationship with your faculty academic mentor enriched your learning experience as a doctoral student?
- Have you found any characteristic of your faculty academic mentor to be problematic?

Today's Business Application:
- To understand the benefits of a positive academic mentor-mentee relationship during the dissertation writing process for some women in educational leadership roles.
- To help higher education conceptualize the likely benefits for females leaders who acquire an academic mentor when navigating the dissertation writing process.
- To help higher education become more aware of the need for more effective levels of support for females in leadership roles when navigating through the dissertation writing process.

REFERENCES

Association of American Colleges Project on the Status and Education of Women. (1983). *Academic mentoring for women students and faculty: A new look at an old way to get ahead.* Washington, DC: U.S. Department of Education.

Blair, C., & Haworth, J. (1999, November). Doctoral student attrition and persistence: A meta-synthesis of research. Paper presented at the Annual Meeting of the Association for the Study of Higher Education. San Antonio-TX (ERIC Document Reproduction Service No. ED 437008).

Bloom, G., Castagna, C., Moir, E., & Warren, B. (2005). *Blended coaching.* Thousand Oaks, CA: Corwin Press.

Butin, D. (2010). *The education dissertation: A guide for practitioner scholars.* Thousand Oaks, CA: Corwin.

Cofield, N. (2016). *Why it's so difficult for minority women to find mentors.* Retrieved from http://www.fastcompany.com/3040341/strong-female-lead/why-its-so-difficult-for-minority

Cohen, L. (2011). *The handy psychology answer book.* Canton, MI: Visible Ink Press.

Council of Graduate Schools Ph.D Completion Project. (2008). *Ph.D completion project.* Washington, DC: Council of Graduate Schools.

Crawford, C. (2010). *Manager's guide to mentoring.* New York, NY: McGraw Hill.

Creswell, J. (2012). *Educational research: Planning, conducting, and evaluating quantitative and qualitative research.* Boston, MA: Pearson.

Foss, S., & Waters, W. (2007). *Destination dissertation.* Latham, MD: Rowman & Littlefield Publisher.

Fullan, M. (2014). *The principal: Three keys to maximizing impact.* San Francisco, CA: Jossey-Bass.

Gardiner, M., Enomoto, E., & Grogan, M. (2000). *Mentoring women into school leadership: Coloring outside the lines.* Albany, NY: State University of NY Press.

Gardner, S. (2008). What's too much and what's too little?: The process of becoming an independent researcher in doctoral education. *The Journal of Higher Education, 79,* 326–350. doi:10.1353/jhe.0.0007

Holmes, B., Danner, D., Gibson, J., & Woods, E. (2016). An audacious agenda: Creating thought leaders and new knowledge creators from the profession. *Clute International Academic Conference* (pp. 1–13). Washington, DC: Clute Institute.

Maher, M., Ford, M., & Thompson, C. (2004). Degree progress of women doctoral students: Factors that constrain, facilitate, and differentiate. *The Review of Higher Education,* 385–408. 10.1353/rhe.2004.0003

Neblett, J. (2004). *Informal mentoring of minority women in business settings.* Boca Raton, FL: Dissertation.com.

Peters, A. (2003). *A case study of an African American principal participating in an administrative leadership academy.* Columbus, OH: The Ohio State University.

Pride, M. (2005). *The journey through the dissertation writing process: Do relationships matter?* (Unpublished doctoral dissertation) Retrieved from Michigan State University-East Lansing.

Putsche, L., Storrs, D., Lewis, A., & Haylett, J. (2008).The development of a mentoring program for university undergraduate women. *Cambridge Journal of Education, 38,* 513–528. doi:10.1080/03057640802482322

Pyke, R. (2010). *Benefits of mentoring female doctoral students.* Beau Bassin Mauritius: VDM Publishing House Ltd. *Permission granted to use interview questions and other pertinent information.

Salem, R. (2003, July). Empathic Listening. Retrieved from http://www.beyondintractabiliity.org.

Tinto, V. (2007). Research and practice of student retention: What's next? *The Journal of College Student Retention, 8*(1), 1–19. doi:10.2190/4YNU-4TMB-22DJ-AN4W

University College Dublin. (2016, March 22). *UCD Academic mentoring principles underpinning mentoring.* Retrieved from www.ucd.ie/mentor/principlesunderpinningmentoring/.

University of Washington. (2015, April 2). *University of Washington Human Resources.* Retrieved from Career Development-Mentee Guide: Managing a successful mentoring relationship: http://www.washington.edu/admin/hr/roles/ee/careerdev/mentoring/manage-relationship.htm

U.S. Army. (n.d.). *Mentorship guide.* Retrieved from http://www.quartermaster.army.mil/oqmg/warrant_officer_proponency/Mentorship_Program/GUIDE/Table_of_Contents.htm

Wallce, D. (n.d.). *Critical connections: Meaningful mentoring relationships between women doctoral students and their dissertation chairpersons.* Baton Rouge, LA: Unpublished doctoral dissertation, Louisiana State University andd Agriculture and Mechanical College.

About the Author . . .

Dr. Kathi Harrington Gibson, a native of Richmond County, North Carolina, matriculated through the following universities: UNC-Chapel Hill (BA degree in English Education); UNC-Pembroke (MA Degree in Educational Administration and Supervision); University of South Carolina, Columbia, SC (Doctorate in the Philosophy of Educational Leadership; Cognate- School Social Work). Dr. Kathi's professional career, which spans three decades, began as a public school English teacher, and evolved to: Assistant Principal, Principal, Educational Supervisor, Director of Curriculum and Instruction, Assistant Superintendent, Associate Superintendent, and Superintendent of Schools.

The highlights of her professional career include professional accomplishments in Cumberland County, Fayetteville, North Carolina. From 1998–2003, Kathi served as an Assistant Superintendent for Student Services, and an Associate Superintendent for Curriculum and Instructional Programs. Continuing her professional career, Kathi was chosen as the Superintendent of Schools for Weldon City Schools and Northampton County Schools.

In 2008, Dr. Kathi retired from the superintendency and initiated her very own consulting business, which she calls *K-Konsult International*. Her consultations have ranged from: (a) International Teacher Recruitment, (b) School Age Specialist for After-School Programs across the state of NC, (c) Professional Development specialist for Day Care Centers, and (d) Mentorship of Principals in the state of South Carolina. Presently, Dr. Kathi spends her weeks mentoring curriculum staff. Kathi is an adjunct faculty member at Gardner-Webb University in Boiling Springs, NC and teaches graduate level courses in the departments of Educational Leadership and Curriculum and Instruction. Kathi resides in Fayetteville, NC.

To reach Dr. Kathi Gibson for information on professional development coaching, please contact via email: gibson.kathi@gmail.com

3

Using Leadership to Improve Firm Performance through Knowledge Management

Dr. Cynthia J. Young

Throughout 23 years on active duty in the U.S. Navy, first as an enlisted Sailor, then as a Surface Warfare Officer, one concept remained true and that was that as a leader, knowledge management was a key success factor in completing the mission. As a female leader in a male-dominated industry, my use of knowledge management was just as important and necessary as my male counterparts. As a leader, knowing the importance of gaining tacit knowledge based on experiences of others is as important as sharing knowledge. Knowing how to use the tacit knowledge one has gained as well as using explicit knowledge teaches the skills of thinking innovatively and determining solutions as required to meet the tasking given. Within this chapter, actionable recommendations are provided for organizations to better support women in leadership positions as well as employees without *leader* or *manager* in their title for prevention of knowledge loss, while increasing firm performance and improving organizational knowledge management practices.

Knowledge management is a fundamental success factor for firm performance of the U.S. ship repair industry in support of the military. Because of the many configurations within the maintenance and modernization requirements of 45 East Coast surface ships (Navy Chief of Information, 2015), the learning curves in the ship repair industry rely on knowledge management practices (Young, 2016). With this large potential for lack of continuity and management of knowledge, the goal of the study was to examine the relationship of knowledge management and innovation on firm performance (Young, 2016). The specific problem was the lack of clarity whether or not the ship repair managers in the mid-Atlantic region understood the relationship of knowledge management and innovation on firm performance in their industry (Young, 2016).

Organizations should account for risks by extending or breaking through the boundaries for performance improvement without gender biases. Knowledge management is not limited to software or by gender. Management of organizational knowledge supports the capabilities of the organization and the organization's entire workforce from Chief Executive Officer (CEO) to the junior employee through (a) employee development; (b) education and training; and (c) sharing best practices in addition to the use of communication media (Basu, 2014).

The requirements of knowledge management are similar in all organizations regardless of the industry. If organizational knowledge is not managed properly by leadership, male or female, organizational knowledge is lost or filed away. At a minimum, the U.S. military ensures knowledge management through (a) recognized best practices, (b) lessons learned databases, (c) standard operating procedures (SOP), (d) pass down logs, (e) mentorship, and (f) training at regular intervals. Leaders and managers use these tools to manage knowledge through employee turnover within the organization for ensuring a stable state of firm performance. As military leaders, the expectation is that male and female leaders support, encourage, and enable knowledge management practices for the betterment of the command and mission accomplishment. When we do not take the previous knowledge learned into account, we end up with lessons relearned, which accomplishes nothing.

Using Leadership to Improve Firm Performance Through Knowledge Management

Corporate knowledge sharing occurs through employee communication (Young, 2016). Management of organizational knowledge supports the outcome of firm performance, whether individual-to-individual or team-to-team. Organizations may be experiencing a lack of continuity and management of knowledge due to decreasing workforce labor since 1992 (Bureau of Labor Statistics, 2014). Between 1992 and 2012, a reduction in the labor force occurred with workers aged 25 to 64 of 6.1% with an expected projected decline by 2.2% resulting in a remaining 63.1% of the total labor force (Bureau of Labor Statistics, 2014). Organizations must have methods to maintain knowledge and innovative practices in support of positive firm performance (Young, 2016). With this noted decrease in labor force, I conducted a quantitative correlation study to examine the relationship for a correlation between knowledge management, innovation, and firm performance (Young, 2016).

Leadership within an organization is an influence on knowledge exploration, exploitation, and innovation (Donate & Guadamillas, 2011). Two of the most recognized types of leadership support the organizational influence: transformational and transactional. Transformational leadership involves personal interaction to stimulate intellectual thought (Antonakis & House, 2014; Tse, Huang, & Lam, 2013). Transactional leadership involves self-interest relationship between the leader and the workforce (Strom, Sears, & Kelly, 2014). The use of transformational and transactional depends on the situation, as well as individually dependent based on the interaction between leaders and the individuals within the workforce. Strategic leadership differs from transactional leadership because of leadership's deference of individual needs and non-inspirational relationship (Antonakis & House, 2014). Cuadradro, Garcia-Ael, and Molero (2015) found through a study on gender biases that masculine traits were valued over female traits in managerial roles.

Organizations must determine how leadership can make a difference in management of knowledge without assigning gender biases in knowledge management. Removing bias in support of women in leadership positions must include ensuring organizations assess and remove any status differential in gender stereotyping (Bruckmuller, Hegarty, & Abele, 2012). As a group, women in leadership positions may experience a lessened influence based on their perceived status and power (Bruckmuller et al., 2012), which may lessen the acceptance of their knowledge and management of organizational knowledge.

Theoretical Foundation

Through consideration of three theoretical frameworks, there were differing aspects of learning and knowledge management in which organizations found necessary for quality firm performance. The frameworks considered were (a) the organizational learning theory in which Argote and Miron-Spector (2011) theorized organizational learning occurred through an environmental context with a latent organizational context with member experiences and organizational tools; (b) Calantone, Cavusgil, and Zhao's (2002) framework of learning orientation, innovation, and performance; and (c) Nonaka, Toyama, and Konno's (2000) unified model of dynamic knowledge creation. The theoretical framework most appropriate for this study was the unified model of dynamic knowledge creation by Nonaka et al. Nonaka et al. incorporated the concept of socialization, externalization, combination, and internalization (SECI); *ba,* a location of physical, virtual, or mental properties used as a place to share knowledge; and leadership as the foundation of the theoretical framework.

The unified model of dynamic knowledge creation complemented the independent and dependent variables under examination. The study extended the SECI concept through the whole of knowledge management. Innovation practices supported the concept of *ba* because innovation occurs in a place both virtually and physical. Organizational leadership ensured firm performance is improved, extended, and supported throughout the organization. Based on these relationships, this theoretical framework worked best for this study.

Throughout the literature review, I addressed various aspects of knowledge management, innovation, firm performance. The study also addressed the concepts of learning organizations, innovation culture, and employee turnover. Using the unified model of dynamic knowledge creation best supported this purpose of the examination of the relationship between knowledge management and innovation on firm performance (Nonaka et al., 2000). Although leadership is a primary aspect of the unified model of dynamic knowledge creation, Nonaka et al. (2000) did not distinguish between male and female leaders.

Literature Review

A learning organization reflects more than just teaching because these institutions represent management of knowledge as part of the organizational culture that occurs throughout the workforce (Young, 2016). Organizational leaders manage knowledge through venues such as communities of practice (Musa & Ismail, 2011), virtual or Cloud communities (Sultan, 2013), and both knowledge-in-practice (McIver, Lengnick-Hall, Lengnick-Hall, & Ramachandran, 2013; Nilsen, Nordström, & Ellström, 2012) and knowledge-intensive firms (Casimir, Lee, & Loon, 2012). These venues are important, because they allow a selection of knowledge management styles that best match the organizational culture and the employees within the respective organizations. Becoming a learning organization also allows leadership to match knowledge management practices with their employees' learning styles.

Sectors of knowledge management include (a) capture, (b) creation, (c) transfer, and (d) sharing. The unified model of dynamic knowledge creation supports the importance of the different phases of knowledge management, primarily knowledge creation, through the SECI spiral development process as (a) socialization (tacit-to-tacit) to externalization (tacit-to-explicit), (b) externalization (tacit-to-explicit) to combination (explicit-to-explicit), (c) combination (explicit-to-explicit) to internalization (explicit-to-tacit), and (d) internalization (explicit-to-tacit) back to socialization (tacit-to-tacit) (Nonaka, 1994; Nonaka et al., 2000). These four phases of knowledge creation occur through the different *ba*s, or places of knowledge creation such as the previously described learning organization (Von Krogh, Nonaka, & Rechsteiner, 2012).

The integration of knowledge creation throughout the organization may support a culture of innovation within the organization (Nonaka, 1994; Nonaka & Konno, 1998). The knowledge creation occurs because of the interaction between the different phases in which people convert tacit knowledge to explicit knowledge and back again to tacit knowledge and so on (Nonaka, 1994; Nonaka et al., 2000). Understanding that the spiral of knowledge creation does not start or end in any of specific SECI phases to support capturing, transferring, and sharing of knowledge throughout an organization is critical for leaders and managers in the use of organizational knowledge management. It is also important to recognize the importance of communication in the knowledge management processes and that a lack of communication may halt knowledge the sectors of knowledge management.

An innovation culture supports critical thinking (Musa & Ismail, 2011), which is important to realize because employees use cross-organizational knowledge in support of innovative ideas (Ganco, 2013). Knowledge creation facilitates organizational innovation

(Sankowska, 2013). Crespi and Zuniga (2012) studied the relationship of innovation and productivity and found that knowledge supported increased productivity of innovative practices. With this relationship, work engagement leads to psychological empowerment (Bhatnagar, 2012). Sharifirad and Ataei (2012) found through a qualitative study exploring organizational and innovation culture of Iranian automobile companies that a culture of employee empowerment increased innovation commitment and participation. The empowerment of employees may grow as the organizational culture supports knowledge management and innovation.

As employee turnover occurs, leaders must ensure they, at a minimum, maintain firm performance through knowledge transfer (Musa & Ismail, 2011). Knowledge retention must be a consideration of an organization's strategic plan in combatting employee turnover and it is up to the leadership to guide the organization in knowledge retention efforts. Employee turnover yields different results regarding knowledge sharing based on whether the turnover is voluntary such as a resignation (Park & Shaw, 2013) or involuntary such as a firing (Hom, Mitchell, Lee, & Griffeth, 2012) or downsizing (Munoz-Bullon & Sanchez-Bueno, 2014). Whether the employee turnover is voluntary or involuntary, leadership must ensure they are prepared for some level of knowledge loss (Young, 2016). Prevention of knowledge loss during employee turnover remains challenging depending on the relationship between the leaders and the workforce. An organization must be ready to address or deter knowledge loss through strategic planning of their knowledge management.

The organization's ability to (a) increase market share, (b) operate efficiently, and (c) support process or service improvements was the basis of firm performance (Chang & Chuang, 2011; Damanpour & Aravind, 2012; Wang & Wang, 2012). Concerning tacit knowledge sharing, Wang and Wang (2012) found a statistically significant relationship between tacit knowledge sharing, innovation quality, and firm performance, both financial and operational. Wang and Wang's (2012) findings indicated the importance of knowledge management and innovation on firm performance. Throughout an organization, individuals hold the tacit knowledge, which Cohen and Olsen (2015) determined was an organization's human capital.

Survey Instrument

Lopez-Nicolas and Merono-Cerdan (2011) developed a survey questionnaire using questions from (a) Choi and Lee (2002) for knowledge management strategy; (b) Lee and Choi (2003) for innovation' and (c) a combination of firm performance questions from Choi and Lee (2002). Lopez-Nicolas and Merono-Cerdan created this survey, the Strategic Knowledge Management, Innovation, and Performance Questionnaire, in support of conducting empirical testing of 310 Spanish firms to determine knowledge management strategic effects on innovation and firm performance. As with Lopez-Nicolas and Merono-Cerdan, I used survey responses recorded on a Likert-type scale of 1 (*strongly disagree*) through 7 (*strongly agree*). The scale was 1 = *strongly disagree*, 2 = *disagree*, 3 = *somewhat disagree*, 4 = *neither agree nor disagree*, 5 = *somewhat agree*, 6 = *agree*, and 7 = *strongly agree*.

Eight knowledge management questions, two innovation questions, and 10 firm performance questions comprised the questionnaire. The innovation and firm performance questions required answers based on the opinions of the participants based on their view of their organizations and their competition, while the participants responded to the knowledge management questions based on their views of their only organization. None of the responses required access to historic data. Based on the data from the participants' opinions and recollections of their experiences, the study included conclusions and recommendations for actions organizations for improving firm performance as well as the knowledge management and innovation practices.

Data Analysis

Using a quantitative correlational design, the study included examination of knowledge management and innovation on firm performance. Through a questionnaire regarding knowledge management, innovation, and firm performance created by Lopez-Nicholas and Merono-Cerdan (2011), I surveyed members of the Virginia Ship Repair Association, specifically CEOs / presidents, human resource (HR) personnel, and members in leadership positions (Young, 2016). As of 2013, 24.9% of private employment of the shipbuilding and ship repair industry was in Virginia and was 12% larger than the next largest private employing state for shipbuilding and ship repair (Maritime Administration, 2013). The study required a minimum of 68 completed surveys to conduct the data analysis via an a priori power analysis. Following 5 weeks of data collection via an online survey sent to 649 members of 253 VSRA organizations, I received 69 completed surveys (Young, 2016).

Findings

After processing the data using multiple linear regression analysis, I found knowledge management and innovation predicted resultant firm performance (Young, 2016). The linear combination of the two independent variables, knowledge management and innovation, accounted for 34% of the variation of the dependent variable, firm performance (Young, 2016). Knowledge management was a stronger predictor of firm performance than innovation on firm performance (Young, 2016). This finding held no surprises because innovation uses both tacit and explicit knowledge for product and process improvements. As with the factor of leadership in Nonaka's et al. (2000) unified model of dynamic knowledge creation, the study did not distinguish between male and female leaders, therefore, there was no distinction of responses between male and female leaders who comprised the participants of CEO / Presidents, HR personnel, or members in leadership positions within the organizations.

Other than one knowledge management responses, no questions had a mean response above 6 (*agree*) (Young, 2016). The knowledge management mean response for "Results of projects and meetings should be documented in your company" was 6.275 (Young, 2016) and was not a true indicator of the organizational performance, but an opinion-based question on how knowledge management should be conducted. The response signified this question was the highest priority of the knowledge management questions. The next highest mean response in knowledge management was for "Informal dialogues and meetings are used for knowledge sharing in your company" at 5.768 (Young, 2016). The importance of recognizing that none of the knowledge management response means rated below 5.087 suggested the respondents agreed with how they perceived their organizations conducted knowledge management (Young, 2016).

Regarding organizational innovation, participants provided their opinions on if their organizational new or improved products and services were superior to the average in their industry (Lopez-Nicolas & Merono-Cerdan, 2011). The mean score for this question was 4.503 (Young, 2016). The second question the respondents opined on whether their organizations' number of new or improved processes was superior to the average in their industry (Lopez-Nicolas and Merono-Cerdan, 2011). This resulted in a mean response of 4.609 (Young, 2016). Because the required responses were opinion-based, there may have been a different result on the relationship with firm performance if survey responses used historic data.

Similar to the innovation questions, the participants provided their opinion-based responses to the questions regarding firm performance. Ten firm performance questions extended from comparison questions on growth rate through creativity and innovation of employees (Lopez-Nicolas and Merono-Cerdan, 2011). Means of the responses ranged from 4.594 to 5.812 (Young, 2016). Again, as with the innovation results, the findings may have been different if historic data had been used as opposed to opinion-based responses.

Future Research

Because the study used opinion-based responses for this study, it would be interesting to conduct a quantitative correlation study using historic data or by surveying only knowledge managers and innovation leaders (Young, 2016). Although the confidentiality agreement of the study ensured participants had no fear of reprisal in their responses, there was no way to remove all internal angst in responding negatively. A quantitative correlation study using historic data or through surveying only knowledge managers and innovation leaders may provide a fact-based depiction of the relationship, between knowledge management, innovation, and firm performance (Young, 2016). A further division of male and female leader participants may also yield additional insight into the relationships of knowledge management and innovation on firm performance.

Another option to extend the findings of this study is through conducting a qualitative case study to explore perceived successes and failures of small, medium, and large organizations in United States ship repair (Young, 2016). The next option is to explore an organization as a longitudinal study beginning with the detection of deteriorating firm performance through implementation of a strategic plan and examination of the updated firm performance results. A final possibility is to shift to a U.S. ship repair industry that supports the military in another region such as on the West Coast (Young, 2016).

Actionable Recommendations for Leaders

Knowledge management and innovation processes and procedures need to be known or available throughout the organization to support maintaining or improving firm performance (Young, 2016). If organizational leadership shares processes and policies, management can implement or improve mentorship programs and provide cross-training opportunities to allow tacit knowledge transfer and creation of explicit knowledge (Young, 2016). With dedicated knowledge management practices as part of the organizational culture, the explicit knowledge becomes available for incorporation into organizational standard operating procedures, instructions, and guidance (Young, 2016).

Specific recommendations for action are to consider a mentorship program for all employees to participate in to support open lines of communication within departments and across departmental lines and to conduct organizational training within departments (Young, 2016). Prioritization of training based on departmental requirements would support the strategic goals of the organization without occupying the entire organizational workforce simultaneously (Young, 2016). Knowledge sharing during employee onboarding would allow management an opportunity to set a tract of positive knowledge management and innovation mindset rather than the onboarding as strictly a paperwork drill (Young, 2016). Most importantly is to empower employees with the decision-making. Empowerment does not release leadership of the accountability, but does share some of the risk and responsibility, which would help to build leaders as well as to strengthen the overall firm performance incorporating this level of trust into the organizational culture.

Conclusion

Organizations need to remain focused on the strategic goals leading to positive firm performance. The labor force is trending on continued decreases of the workforce aged of 25 to 54 until at least 2022 (Bureau of Labor Statistics, 2014), which may lead to loss of both tacit and explicit organizational knowledge if not addressed. Study results indicated a statistically significant relationship between knowledge management, innovation, and firm performance (Young, 2016). Leaders ensure that the workforce understands knowledge management and innovative practices in support of an organizations goals and objective, or as the military workforce often refers to it, in support of the mission. Continued examination and exploration of this topic in this industry would support the United States ship repair industry and improve the operational availability of the Navy's surface ships.

Knowledge is managed by all within the organization, but leaders shape the knowledge management to support the strategic efforts and overall firm performance improvements. Knowledge management reaches each employee through different aspects of the organization. Gender should not be delineation of the knowledge management efforts. It is the responsibility of organizational leadership to remove gender biases and ensure both men and women are held as equals in the spiral of the dynamic knowledge creation, prevention of knowledge loss during employee departures, and in the mentorship of employees to support knowledge sharing and transfer. These efforts will result in positive growth of organizational firm performance and leadership of knowledge management throughout the organization emphasizing leadership is found at all levels of an organization rather than just those with *leader* or *manager* in the title.

THOUGHTS FROM THE ACADEMIC ENTREPRENEUR

The problem to be solved:

- Improving the influence of leadership of knowledge management throughout an organization.

The goals:

- Understanding how to use leadership for managing knowledge as an organization improving firm performance.
- Understanding how employee empowerment benefits knowledge management throughout an organization.

The questions to ask:

- How can organizational leadership ensure knowledge retention when employees depart the organization?
- How can organizations empower employees to use their tacit knowledge to improve firm performance while making it explicit knowledge?
- What can organizations do to prevent gender biases from affecting firm performance?

Today's Business Application:

- Effective leaders who understand how to manage knowledge while leading their employees to use knowledge innovatively will have more options as solution providers and improve their firm performance.
- Becoming a learning organization supports knowledge retention during employee departures.
- Removal of gender biases in organizational culture may increase firm performance.

REFERENCES

Antonakis, J., & House, R. J. (2014). Instrumental leadership: Measurement and extension of transformational-transactional leadership theory. *Leadership Quarterly, 25,* 746–771. doi:10.1016/j.leaqua.2014.04.005

Argote, L., & Miron-Spektor, E. (2011). Organizational learning: From experience to knowledge. *Organization Science, 22,* 1123–1137. doi:10.1287/orsc.1100.0621

Bhatnagar, J. (2012). Management of innovation: Role of psychological empowerment, working engagement, and turnover intention in the Indian context. *International Journal of Human Resource Management, 23,* 928–951. doi:10.1080/09585192.2012.651313

Basu, R. (2014). Managing quality in projects: An empirical study. *International Journal of Project Management, 32,* 178–187. doi:10.1016/j.ijproman.2013.02.003

Bruckmuller, S., Hegarty, P., & Abele, A. E. (2012). Framing gender differences: Linguistic normativity affects perceptions of power and gender stereotypes. *European Journal of Social Psychology, 42,* 210–218. doi:10.1002/ejsp.858

Bureau of Labor Statistics. (2014). *TED: The economics daily.* Retrieved from http://www.bls.gov/opub/ted/2014/ted_20140124.htm

Calantone, R. J., Cavusgil, S. T., & Zhao, Y. (2002). Learning organization, firm innovation capability, and firm performance. *Industrial Marketing Management, 31,* 515–524. doi:10.1016/S0019-8501(01)00203-6

Casimir, G., Lee, K., & Loon, M. (2012). Knowledge sharing: Influences of trust, commitment, and cost. *Journal of Knowledge Management, 16,* 740–753. doi:10.1108/13673271211262781

Chang, T. C., & Chuang, S. H. (2011). Performance implications of knowledge management processes: Examining the roles of infrastructure capability and business strategy. *Expert Systems with Applications, 38,* 6170–6178. doi:10.1016/j.eswa.2010.11.053

Choi, B., & Lee, H. (2002). Knowledge management strategy and its link to knowledge creation process. *Expert Systems with Applications, 23,* 173–187. doi:10.1016/S0957-4174(02)00038-6

Cohen, J. F., & Olsen, K. (2015). Knowledge management capabilities and firm performance: A test of universalistic, contingency, and complementarity perspectives. *Expert Systems with Applications, 42,* 1178–1188. doi:10.1016/j.eswa.2014.09.002

Crespi, G., & Zuniga, P. (2012). Innovation and productivity: Evidence from six Latin American countries. *World Development, 40,* 273–290. doi:10.1016/j.worlddev.2011.07.010

Cuadrado, I., Garcia-Ael, C., & Molero, F. (2015). Gender-typing of leadership: Evaluations of real and ideal managers. *Scandinavian Journal of Psychology, 56*, 236–244. doi:10.1111/sjop.12187

Damanpour, F., & Aravind, D. (2012). Managerial innovation: Conceptions, processes, and antecedents. *Management and Organization Review, 8*, 423–454. doi:10.1111/j.1740-8784.2011.00233.x

Donate, M. J., & Guadamillas, F. (2011). Organizational factors to support knowledge management and innovation. *Journal of Knowledge Management, 15*, 890–914. doi:10.1108/13673271111179271

Ganco, M. (2013). Cutting the Gordian knot: The effect of knowledge complexity on employee mobility and entrepreneurship. *Strategic Management Journal, 34*, 666–686. doi:10.1002/smj.2044

Hom, P. W., Mitchell, T. R., Lee, T. W., & Griffeth, R. W. (2012). Reviewing employee turnover: Focusing on proximal withdrawal states and an expanded criterion. *Psychological Bulletin, 138*, 831–858. doi:10.1037/a0027983

Lee, H., & Choi, B. (2003). Knowledge management enablers, processes, and organizational performance: An integrative view and empirical examination. *Journal of Management Information Systems, 20*, 179–228. doi:10.1080/07421222.2003.11045756

López-Nicolás, C, & Meroño-Cerdán, Á. L. (2011). Strategic knowledge management, innovation, and performance. *International Journal of Information Management, 31*, 502–509. doi:10.1016/j.ijinfomgt.2011.02.003

Maritime Administration. (2013). *The economic importance of the U.S. shipbuilding and repairing industry.* Retrieved from http://www.marad.dot.gov/documents/MARAD_Econ_Study_Final_Report_2013.pdf

McIver, D., Lengnick-Hall, C., Lengnick-Hall, M., & Ramachandran, I. (2013). Understanding work and knowledge management from a knowledge-in-practice perspective. *Academy of Management Review, 4*, 597–620. doi:10.5465/amr.2011.0266

Munoz-Bullon, F., & Sanchez-Bueno, M. J. (2014). Institutional determinants of downsizing. *Human Resource Management Journal, 24*, 111–128. doi:10.1111/1748-8583.12017

Musa, M. A., & Ismail, S. E. (2011). Governance structure and the creativity and innovation process. *International Journal of Interdisciplinary Social Sciences, 6*, 231–238. Retrieved from http://www.SocialSciences-Journal.com

Navy Chief of Information. (2015). *U.S. Navy ships.* Retrieved from http://www.navy.mil/navydata/our_ship.asp

Nilsen, P., Nordström, G., & Ellström, P.-E. (2012). Integrating research-based and practice-based knowledge through workplace reflection. *Journal of Workplace Learning, 24*, 403–415. doi:10.1108/13665621211250306

Nonaka, I. (1994). A dynamic theory of organizational knowledge creation. *Organization Science, 5,* 14–37. Retrieved from http://orgsci.journal.informs.org

Nonaka, I., & Konno, N. (1998). The concept of "ba": Building a foundation for knowledge creation. *California Management Review, 40,* 40–54. doi:10.2307/41165942

Nonaka, I., Toyama, R., & Konno, N. (2000). SECI, *ba,* and leadership: A unified model of dynamic knowledge creation. *Long Range Planning, 33,* 5–34. Retrieved from http://www.elsevier.com/locate/lrp

Park, T.-Y., & Shaw, J. D. (2013). Turnover rates and organizational performance: A meta-analysis. *Journal of Applied Psychology, 98,* 268–309. doi:10.1037/a0030723

Sankowska, A. (2013). Relationships between organizational trust, knowledge transfer, knowledge creation, and firm's innovativeness. *Learning Organization, 20,* 85–100. doi:10.1108/09696471311288546

Sharifirad, M. S., & Ataei, V. (2012). Organizational culture and innovation culture: Exploring the relationships between constructs. *Leadership and Organization Development Journal, 33,* 494–517. doi:10.1108/01437731211241274

Strom, D. L., Sears, K. L., & Kelly, K. M. (2014). Work engagement: The roles of organizational justice and leadership style in predicting engagement among employees. *Journal of Leadership and Organizational Studies, 21,* 71–82. doi:10.1177/1548051813485437

Sultan, N. (2013). Knowledge management in the age of cloud computing and Web 2.0: Experiencing the power of disruptive innovations. *International Journal of Information Management, 33,* 160–165. doi:10.1016/j.ijinfomgt.2012.08.006

Tabachnick, B. G., & Fidell, L. S. (2013). Multiple regression: Limitations to regression analyses. *Using multivariate statistics* (6th ed.) (pp. 122–128). New Jersey: Pearson Education, Inc.

Tse, H. H. M., Huang, X., & Lam, W. (2013). Why does transformational leadership matter for employee turnover? A multi-foci social exchange perspective. *Leadership Quarterly, 24,* 763–776. doi:10.1016/j.leaqua.2013.07.005

Von Krogh, G., Nonaka, I., & Rechsteiner, L. (2012). Leadership in organizational knowledge creation: A review and framework. *Journal of Management Studies, 49,* 240–277. doi:10.1111/j.1467-6486-2010.00978.x

Wang, Z., & Wang, N. (2012). Knowledge sharing, innovation, and firm performance. *Expert Systems with Applications, 39,* 8899–8908. doi:10.1016/j.eswa.2012.02.017

Young, C. J. (2016). *Knowledge management and innovation on firm performance of United States ship repair* (Doctoral dissertation). Retrieved from ProQuest Dissertations and Theses database. (UMI No. 10042541)

About the Author...

Dr. Cynthia J. Young resides in Chesapeake, Virginia. Dr. Cindy holds several accredited degrees; a Bachelor of Arts (BA) in English Language and Literature from the University of Maryland, College Park; two Masters of Business Administration (MBA), one in e-commerce and one in advanced management studies, from Touro University International; and a Doctorate of Business Administration (DBA) from Walden University.

Dr. Cindy is a Knowledge Manager with McKean Defense, a defense contracting company, after retiring as a Surface Warfare Officer with 23 years in the U.S. Navy. She is a past-Chair of American Society for Quality Tidewater Section 1128, and a member of the Project Management Institute, Golden Key International Honor Society, and Delta Mu Delta International Business Honor Society.

Dr. Cindy holds professional certifications as a Project Management Professional and a Lean Six Sigma Master Black Belt. Her doctoral study, *Knowledge Management and Innovation on Firm Performance of United States Ship Repair,* provided her the opportunity to gain additional professional and academic expertise to facilitate improvements in organizational knowledge management.

To reach Dr. Cynthia J. Young for information on consulting or doctoral coaching, please e-mail: drcynthiajyoung@gmail.com

4

Native American Women in Leadership Working toward a Sustainable Future

Dr. Janie Hall

Background of Leader Strategies Toward Tribal Economic and Stability

The application of refractive thinking includes the tribal gaming industry, which is a race within a culture in a for-profit entity. Yani-de-Soriano et al. (2012) performed a study of online gambling. Yani-de-Soriano et al. found marketing tactics compounded harm to online gamblers and online gaming companies chose profits over harm prevention. The tribal gaming leaders applied refractive thinking and identified eight skills they use toward a sustainable future; their efforts led to economic development and stability. One characteristic of a leadership strategy is the necessity to provide the core values of the business.

Business leaders should be responsive to the needs of their stakeholders through ethically, philanthropically, and societal lenses (Abugre, 2014). Situational leadership theory (SLT) could aid Corporate Social Responsibility (CSR) and may influence organizations by accurate identification of the organization and govern efficacious adoption factors. The exploration of the essential strategies for leader choices could have a substantial influence on existing and future societal needs in the tribal gaming industry.

Thirteen tribal gaming leaders participated in the individual interview and focus group sessions; ten were men and three women in northeast Oklahoma. The objective is to recognize the benefits and limitations of leader roles that will assist the organization. Men and women leaders actively participate in the decisions made by the tribal gaming organization. The focus of the chapter is women in leadership; many women leaders are in Native American culture (Hoxie & Iverson, 1998). Native American women were collaborators, became colonial administrators, and had powerful roles equal to men in the early 1800s (Gillespie, 2014).

Overview of the Study

Organizational leaders attempt to reduce the eco-footprint of the organization and concentrate on the total business value (Coulson-Thomas, 2013). Leadership contributes to the success of international business in most cases (Littrell, 2013). Situational leadership could aid CSR and may influence companies by correct identification of the corporation and determining successful adoption factors. The identification of the gaps may aid leaders in building relationships among organizations (Littrell, 2013). The leader strategies and methods of CSR are processes that might support strategic components. Organizational leaders must act upon the fundamental components to adapt sustainability to survive the long-term future of tribal gaming.

Leaders found a positive link between effective leadership styles and CSR for the good of the community (Du, Swaen, Lindgreen, & Sen, 2013). Organizational leaders encompass the tridimensional CSR business model; however, leader participation could deliver prosperous methods to moderate issues management, environmental management, and stakeholder management (Forte, 2013). The processes leaders adopt may support sustainability and may aid in the industries' survival. The results of the research contributes to a profound perception of the capacity that leaders play in daily judgments and CSR for future generations. The principle issue explored in the case study was the essential leader tools that leaders defined as motivators in CSR. The second issue explored is the motivation of Native American women to become leaders.

The leader strategies and methods of CSR are processes that might support strategic components. Organizational leaders processes improve organizational outcomes and good CSR practices (Du et al., 2013). Native American used emotional intelligence and strategic vision to sell and trade goods they produced on their lands (Hansen & Osterud, 2014). Constructive leaders reduce harm in their efforts to advance CSR approaches for tribal gaming (Yani-de-Soriano, Javed, & Yousafzai, 2012).

Native Americans are loyal to their homeland (Hoxie & Iverson, 1998). The U.S. government created the Dawes Act to allow the sale of tribal reservations to nontribal members (Hansen & Osterud, 2014). Native American women maintained resourcefulness through land ownership (Hansen & Osterud, 2014). Positive community relationships enabled Native American women to participate in the major political events (Hansen & Osterud, 2014). Native American women landowners defended their culture with landownership, which allowed them to maintain the bountiful resources of the land (Hansen & Osterud, 2014).

Tribal gaming is a for-profit organization intended to diminish tribal poverty (Anderson, 2013). Tribal leaders stimulated their resources by introducing gaming quarters on their reservations, which addressed the poverty of tribal members and the neighboring communities (Anderson, 2013). Income changes are beneficial to the tribe (Anderson, 2013). Native American women promoted existence through communication; they were culture bearers, by learning the cultures of the early settlers, and adapting for the welfare of their communities (Gillespie, 2014). Medium and large tribal casinos create a significant net revenue and escalate tribal economy in contrast to smaller tribal casinos (Anderson, 2013).

Sustainable progress is meeting the present needs of society without dwindling resources for future generations (Ameer & Othman, 2012). The increase in community value may improve the well-being of the tribal community (Gillespie, 2014). Native American women and experienced philanthropic opportunities through childcare (Hansen & Osterud, 2014). A woman, known as an honored elder, took risks by bringing value to the tribe in an attempt to change the world (Pesantubbee, 2014). Her motivation was to learn how to make certain foods from the settlers, become an ally, and prevent attacks on her native land (Pesantubbee, 2014)

The inconsistencies between social goals and corporate profits continue to be a relevant issue (Fontaine, 2013). CSR can positively affect communities with socially responsible behaviors (Fontaine, 2013). Organizational leaders realize they need to include CSR in their strategic decisions; different leadership styles have an effect on the outcome of corporate social responsibility (Du et al., 2013). Native American women landowners were resilient during the period of tribal land loss by maintaining the resources of their land, land lease, and through landownership. Organizational leaders should address social responsibility and environmental sustainability through good leadership strategies to improve economic growth, competitiveness, and consumer interest (Fontaine, 2013). The lack of leader strategies used to sustain CSR could reduce the industries' survival.

Conceptual Framework

SLT served as the foundation of the descriptive case study. SLT includes the fundamental concepts to create a better understanding of surroundings, which helps improve business processes (Hersey & Blanchard, 1969). The methods and leader strategies of CSR are behaviors that maintain strategic objectives (Coulson-Thomas, 2013). The issue in this study was the strategies organizational leaders use to include the benefits of CSR within the organization.

The results of the study may contribute to a deeper awareness of the capacity that leaders play in routine judgments and CSR for future generations. The interview questions portrayed whether CSR was the effect of leader initiatives or a manifestation of tribal heritage.

Research Methodology and Design

The leader strategies were explored to determine how to incorporate CSR in the workplace in a descriptive case study. Qualitative research features an open process for the selection of participants (Yin, 2014). Case study research allows an understanding of the multifaceted concerns and accentuates the knowledge of the milieu in a small degree of circumstances and the relationship between events (Yin, 2014). A case study was chosen because of the extensive information and perceptions derived from the participants in the qualitative exploratory case study design.

The data collection and analysis techniques were obtained by voice recording the interviews and inspecting the transcribed interviews to establish the trustworthiness for accuracy. The descriptive case study design incorporated a systematic approach to the uniqueness of the recanted events in detail of the real life experience (Yin, 2014). Phases employed in this type of analysis included research question, interview questions, data collection, data analysis, method, and limitations (Yin, 2014). The purpose of this study was to explore the strategies leaders use to provide CSR processes in the tribal gaming industry.

Data Collection

Tribal gaming leaders in Oklahoma participated in open-ended interviews to build on a conceptual framework of SLT. A snowball sampling strategy was a contingency plan for participants who opt out of the study (Yin, 2014). Prospective leadership participants from the same gaming organization received and responded to an email invitation. Five men and one woman participated in a focus group session; five additional men and two women from participated in individual interview sessions.

The data collection technique included an open-ended interview questioning process to understand the skills tribal gaming leaders use toward sustainability. During each interview, the leaders actions were observed and their responses were ecorded by note taking and audio recordings during the individual and focus group session. The data collection process consisted of leader participation, a review of company documents, including a promotional mailer, press releases, and an internal communication document. The company documents were triangulated with the answers collected through semi-structured interviews and a current literature review to support the research outcomes.

Data Analysis

Qualitative data is easier to manage by categorizing data or coding the data for a deeper perception through thought and reasoning (Yin, 2014). Multiple codes surfaced with the use of the CAQDAS known as Dedoose. A researcher can determine the categories and codes to associate participant replies with the use of predetermined categories or codes of inference and a blend of both (Yin, 2014).

Findings

Eight relevant themes emerged from the initial codes. The study included divisions into the eight relevant themes into four major themes and four minor themes. The major themes included business value, strategic vision, collaboration, and communication.

The minor themes identified were motivation / innovation, emotional intelligence, resilience, and philanthropic opportunity. The relevant themes specified the strategies tribal gaming leaders use toward CSR.

The study included comparisons within the literature review and the conceptual framework with the themes to evaluate the reliability of the study. The conceptual framework theory of SLT aided in the analysis and interpretation of the findings addressed the central research question. The individual replies indicated SLT, which the leadership performance changes as the responsibilities vary (Hersey & Blanchard, 1969). The findings of the study specified that leadership strategies are essential in tribal gaming toward a sustainable future.

A serendipitous theme emerged in the focus group and individual interview sessions. One man and two women leaders explained their perception of CSR. The tribal gaming leaders based their definition on the organization's mission statement. Leaders that lack clarity of CSR allow the efforts to become distorted, which mistakably creates a fragile rationale (Guthey & Morsing, 2014). The implementation of the mission statement provided the leaders with a formal summary of the organizational values. Business value was the top major theme identified by the tribal gaming leaders.

Summary

This descriptive case study contributed to a growing body of knowledge relating to CSR, SLT, and tribal gaming. The purpose of this study was to explore the strategies business leaders use to warrant CSR processes in the tribal gaming industry. Organizations must be strong to implement, initiate, and coordinate CSR actions (Abugre, 2014). Hersey and Blanchard (1969) discussed methods of behavior modification, reinforcement, and extinction in behavioral patterns; the benefits of SLT, which originated on *Ini-*

tiating Structure and *Consideration.* Leader strategies toward CSR can be challenging; yet, may substantiate the mission of the organization. The purpose of this study seems applicable as all leaders attested their observations toward sustainability as they linked to the organization's mission statement.

The results provide four major themes: business value, strategic vision, collaboration, and communication. Data collected from the leaders included four minor themes: motivation and innovation, emotional intelligence, resilience, and philanthropic opportunities. One serendipitous theme augmented the study as two women and one man expressed their perception and meaning of CSR. Organizational leaders notice the economic advantages of CSR based on core values and improved organizational skills (Calabrese, Costa, Menichini, Rosati, & Sanfelice, 2013). Fontaine (2013) discovered value creation, risk management, and corporate philanthropy in the lens of CSR encourages organizational growth and commitment to the communities they serve.

Conclusion

The results of this descriptive case study concluded four major themes: business value, strategic vision, collaboration, and communication. The data analysis yielded four minor themes: motivation and innovation, emotional intelligence, resilience, and philanthropic opportunities. A serendipitous theme was an addition to the study as three of the individuals expressed their perception and meaning of CSR. Organizations have difficulties increasing the knowledge base of good CSR use to a community's population (Dincer & Dincer, 2013).

Native Americans shared an admiration for humankind and value the importance of relationships (Hoxie & Iverson, 1998). The strategies that emerged in this study may help male and female leaders in sustainability in any sector. The top-down bottom-up method can be applied to a particular focus on CSR, leadership, governance, and employee attrition (Low & Ang, 2013). The results of the study promote an innate comprehension of the capacity leaders make in daily judgments and CSR for future generations. An important aspect of the leader strategies is the need to account for the perceptions of the core values of the organization.

There is an opportunity for improved CSR efforts in different sectors. A considerable number of leadership strategies aided tribal gaming leaders in CSR, in particular, business value. The specific challenges identified in this chapter focus on tribal gaming leader strategies toward a sustainable future. Women have the opportunity as leaders. This chapter offered a refractive thinking analysis of Native American women and SLT with the application of best practices and identified skills used toward a sustainable future.

THOUGHTS FROM THE ACADEMIC ENTREPRENEUR

The problem to be solved:
- Business leaders have limited knowledge of strategies used to sustain CSR.

The goals:
- Developing appropriate leader strategies and participation to meet the needs of tribal economic development and stability.
- Understanding the benefits and limitations of leader strategies toward sustainability.

The questions to ask:
- How have women leader roles helped shape Native American culture?
- What empowered Native American women to become leaders?

Today's Business Application:

- Understanding the benefits and limitations of women as leaders in the Native American culture.

- Understanding culture and gender toward a specific leadership style to obtain the best outcome in the lens of sustainability.

- Empowering leaders with factual knowledge of best practices used toward sustainability.

REFERENCES

Abugre, J. (2014). Managerial role in organizational CSR: Empirical lessons from Ghana. *Corporate Governance, 14*, 104–119. doi:10.1108/CG-10-2011-0076

Ameer, R., & Othman, R. (2012). Sustainability practices and corporate financial performance: A study based on the top global corporations. *Journal of Business Ethics, 108*(1), 61–79. doi:10.1007/s10551-011-1063-y

Anderson, R. (2013). Tribal casino impact on American Indians well-being: Evidence from reservation-level census data. *Contemporary Economic Policy, 31*, 291–300. doi:10.1111/j.1465-7287.2011.00300.x

Calabrese, A., Costa, R., Menichini, T., Rosati, F., & Sanfelice, G., (2013). Turning corporate social responsibility-driven opportunities into competitive advantages: A two-dimensional model. *Knowledge and Process Management, 20*(1), 50–58. doi:10.1002/kpm.1401

Coulson-Thomas, C. (2013). Quality leadership for sustainability. *Management Services Journal, 57*(1), 14–18. Retrieved from http://www.ims-productivity.com/page.cfm/content/Management-Services-Journal/

Du, S., Swaen, V., Lindgreen, A., & Sen, S. (2013). The roles of leadership styles in corporate social responsibility. *Journal of Business Ethics, 114*(1), 155–169. doi:10.1007/s10551-012-1333-3

Fontaine, M. (2013). Corporate social responsibility and sustainability: The new bottom line? *International Journal of Business and Social Science, 4*(4), 110–119. Retrieved from http://ijbssnet.com

Gillespie, J. L. (2014). Amerindian women's influence on the colonial enterprise of Spanish Florida. *Southern Quarterly, 51*(4), 85–102. Retrieved from http://sites.usm.edu/southern-quarterly-literary-magazine/

Hansen, K. V., & Osterud, G. (2014). Landowning, dispossession and the significance of land among Dakota and Scandinavian women at Spirit Lake, 1900–1929. *Gender & History, 26*, 105–127. doi:10.1111/1468-0424.12054

Hersey, P., & Blanchard, K. (1969). Life cycle theory of leadership. *Training and Development Journal, 23*(5), 1–34. Retrieved from http://psycnet.apa.org/psycinfo/1970-19661-001

Hoxie, F. E., & Iverson, P. (1998). *Indians in American history: An introduction.* Wheeling, IL: Harlan Davidson.

Littrell, R. F. (2013). Explicit leader behavior: A review of literature, theory development, and research project results. *Journal of Management Development, 32*, 567–605. doi:10.1108/JMD-04-2013-0053

Pesantubbee, M. E. (2014). Nancy Ward: American patriot or Cherokee nationalist? *The American Indian Quarterly, 38*(2), 177–206. Retrieved from http://www.nebraskapress.unl.edu/product/American-Indian-Quarterly,673174.aspx

Yani-de-Soriano, M., Javed, U., & Yousafzai, S. (2012). Can an industry be socially responsible if its products harm consumers? The case of online gambling. *Journal of Business Ethics, 110*, 481–497. doi:10.1007/s10551-012-1495-z

Yin, R. K. (2014). *Applications of case study research (5th ed.).* Thousand Oaks, CA: Sage.

About the Author...

Dr. Janie Hall resides in Joplin, MO. Dr. Janie holds several accredited degrees; a Bachelor of Arts (BA) in Healthcare Management; a Master of Business Administration (MBA) from Ottawa University; and a Doctorate of Business Administration (DBA) from Walden University.

Dr. Janie is a small business owner of JA Hall Consulting and is an Adjunct Faculty Member at Vatterott College, approved to teach business, management, and healthcare related courses. She enjoys the paving a way to academic excellence, interacting with students, and teaching core concepts leading to further investigation. She is a member of Delta Mu Delta, the Golden Key Honour Society, Society of Professional Consultants, and Professional Editors Network (PEN).

Dr. Janie disseminated the findings of her doctoral study, *Tribal Gaming Leaders toward a Sustainable Future*, through, a peer-reviewed article, and multiple speaking engagements. She was awarded the Doctoral Study of the Year Award, 2016. Her study provided the opportunity to gain professional and academic expertise to facilitate improvements in the small and medium-sized businesses.

To reach Dr. Janie Hall for information on consulting or doctoral coaching, please e-mail: janie-hall@hotmail.com or visit her website at www.jahall consulting.com

5

Creating Refractive Thinking in the Classroom to Inspire Accounting Leadership in Women

Dr. Michelle Boese

Classroom influences refractive thinking, preparing students for real-life career sustainability in accounting and leadership roles. Changing a classroom from content related framework themes to interactive student-driven classroom (Inquiry-based learning) empowers students to ask questions, engage in group-settings, nurtures problem solving, and stimulates reflective thinking, critical thinking, and refractive thinking. A flexible environment supports students having an actual voice in the classroom which is the focus of this chapter.

Classroom influences leadership in an Inquiry-based learning flexible environment. Women focus on relationship *between* the parties in a negotiation and men focus on the *outcome* of the negotiation. Students challenged the issues revealed during the negotiations in class and the results completed their exercise. After the exercise, reflective thinking followed with critical thinking and in conclusion refractive thinking as part of a class discussion.

Women influence accounting because they continue to earn more than half of all college degrees in accounting. Introducing real-world accounting issues in class gives the students the opportunity to feel and understand the business atmosphere and the development of talent needed worldwide. Many colleges and universities hold job fairs for students during their school year to introduce subsequent job availability and internships. Inquiry-based classrooms lend to the development of communications, team focus, leadership, problem solving, refractive thinking, and the inspiration of creativity as part of real world application. Giving a team a task in class to resolve and verbally present the outcomes establishes leadership and task-oriented designs with the team determining how the verbal presentation evolves, furthering skills needed and looked for within the business atmosphere.

Additionally, volunteering leads to networking and leadership roles by uniting women and community service through accounting firms that strategically target their volunteer programs within their corporate social responsibility (CSR) area. Targeted volunteering provides women accountants with networking opportunities and the opportunity to develop better networking skills to advance to leadership and partner opportunities in their accounting firms. Volunteering expands careers when women are involved with not-for-profits and community based organizations outside of their immediate career expertise. Ultimately, women enjoy these opportunities to make a difference while working with colleagues and community service volunteering.

Classroom Influences Refractive Thinking

Preparing students for real-life career sustainability in leadership involves more than providing students with content related to framework themes. Inverting the classroom is reversing *professor*-guided classrooms to *student*-driven classrooms (Inquiry-based learning). The Inquiry-based learning model empowers students to ask questions, engage in-group settings, problem solving, and stimulates the mind. The thinking process begins with reflective thinking (relate new knowledge to prior knowledge) then moves to critical thinking (making clear, reasonable judgments) and producing decisions that move beyond traditional thinking is refractive thinking (Prayitno, Subanji, & Muksar, 2016; Colby, Bilics, & Lerch, 2012). An Inquiry-based learning classroom environment supports refractive thinking, giving students an actual voice in the classroom. To demonstrate, students formulate probable solutions to an accounting issue given at the end of their last accounting class. Entering their next accounting class with questions allows the ability to share insights and resolve the issue.

The classroom is the conference room. Each student develops guiding questions outside of class. As each student takes a position on the matter at hand in class, students challenge reflective thinking, critical thinking, and refractive thinking. An Inquiry-based learning model in accounting challenges the refractive thinking mind. The Inquiry-based learning used in the classroom helps to further develop time management skills, creativity, and problem solving to assist in developing networking and leadership roles. Problem solving in accounting practice in the real word is not a pre-set problem; it is a problem situation constructed from materials, which are uncertain and troubling. Thompson and Washington (2015) mentioned that Kitaoka's (2011) study findings show an increase of teacher-student communication when a rich environment of problem solving exists increases student performance.

Teaching using lectures in accounting courses applies the analytical and theory techniques, not the practical application experience. Without refractive thinking, students fail to support critical thinking and problem solving (Reinstein, 2008). An Inquiry-based learning classroom agrees with the thinking of Limbach, Duron, and Waugh (2008) in their five-step process for teaching that includes: (a) learning objectives; (b) teaching through questioning; (c) practicing before assessment; (d) reviewing, refining, and improving; and (e) providing feedback and assessment of learning.

Creating an environment for refractive thinking and leadership in an Inquiry-based learning classroom and relating to accounting practice is a better teaching model to prepare students to be effective and efficient in practicing within the accounting profession. Pfeffer and Fong (2012) commented that competition within universities is from consulting firms providing executive courses in practical use of leadership in the real world. Combining leadership techniques with accounting in an Inquiry-based learning classroom translates to the business accounting language and supports refractive thinking.

Classroom Influences Leadership

Influencing leadership in an Inquiry–based learning classroom creates a real world business environment. The organizational climate within a company directly relates to the business health of a company. Even when an organization uses task-oriented leadership, the organizational climate is a priority. Some leaders in organizations keep a firm focus on their business at hand (task-oriented) and other leaders take into consideration how workers' interactions influences the work environment (relationship-oriented) (Schreiner, 2016). The accounting course is a task-oriented perspective in the classroom and in practice; accounting is more of a relationship-orientation with tasks.

Different communication styles tend to determine different negotiating styles between men and women. Jacobs and Schain (2009) illustrated that women focus on the relationship between the parties and men focus on the outcome of the negotiation. To demonstrate, an exercise handed to the students helps them to formulate a resolution to an accounting problem using small team organization. The students question and answer each other within their groups to begin establishing probable points of discussion and analysis. The lead students then present their findings in negotiation. The female lead students presented in a relationship leadership style and the male students presented their negotiation style on the outcome of the negotiation. An interactive discussion followed on the leadership styles used. The outcome of the discussion is very informative exchange of communication between the students.

More Than Numbers

Accounting is more than numbers. Women's advance into higher-level leadership continues to increase with the increase of women business entrepreneurs. The marketplace statistics shifted with increasing numbers of women as business owners and leadership personnel in organizations continue to seek accounting firms with women in positions of leadership (El-Ramly, 2013). This outcome is a competitive advantage for women in accounting.

In addition, the diversity in the workplace with an increased number of single parents' produced flexible schedules and alternative arrangements that are more attractive to women interested in leadership roles in accounting; accounting firms are accommodating these requests (El-Ramly, 2013). The Women's Initiatives Executive Committee (WIEC) survey found 44% of accounting employees at CPA firms are women (El-Ramly, 2013). The WIEC offers advice for building additional skills in business development, networking, and career management (American Institute of Certified Public Accountants [AICPA], 2016).

The change in the accounting profession that accommodates flexible arrangements continues to make accounting attractive to the younger generation. Accounting classrooms in colleges and universities is the environment for developing such leadership skills. The Inquiry-based learning model used in my classroom gives students opportunities to review real world public accounting reports and the outcomes of those reports.

Accounting Move Project (2012) commented that MIT and Carnegie-Mellon professors conducted research assigning several problem-solving tasks to students with similar IQ's in a classroom. The results showed that more women on the team did better in solving the tasks (Accounting Move Project, 2012). The researchers determined that women dominated teams showed refined social skills in return inspired their group intelligence (Accounting Move Project, 2012).

In addition, the International Federation of Accountants is an avid supporter of the Global Women Leadership Foundation (GWL) that provides accounting articles on global women in accounting leadership. The GWL conducts research worldwide in the development of leadership skills for women in the accounting profession (Zwart, 2014).

Women Influence Accounting

AICPA (2015) research in the supply of accounting graduates and the demand for public accounting recruits confirmed that women in the United States continue to earn more than half of all college degrees in accounting. Women earned 52.1% of bachelor degrees, 52.7% of master degrees, and 44.4% doctoral degrees. Further examinations of women of minorities continue to earn a smaller percentage of college degrees in accounting and related services. Between the years of 2013 and 2014, African American Women, earned 7.5%, Asian women earned 8.1%, and Hispanic / Latina women earned 8.2% in the bachelor degree program in accounting (Catalyst, 2016). In the master degree program, 2.8% are African American women, 4.6% are Asian women, and 3.1% are Hispanic women (Catalyst, 2016).

Women in senior management positions in accounting in the United States rose from 38% in 2011 to 47% in 2015 (AICPA, 2015) and women accountants and auditors reached 63%. Women on management committees grew from 17% in 2011 to 23% in 2015 (AICPA, 2015), while women of minorities employed in accounting in, tax preparation, bookkeeping, and payroll service was 16% in 2015. From a global perspective, the overall percentage of women studying accounting is approximately 50% (AICPA, 2015).

Introducing the same business design of meetings in an accounting class gives the students the opportunity to feel and understand the business atmosphere. Many colleges and universities hold job fairs for students during their school year to introduce job availability and internships as a result.

Firms benefit from community service projects with new leads and business. Accounting Move Project (2012) commented that newly hired women accounting graduates need the least preparation to start working with clients directly. The women graduates are more client-ready and professional directly out of college and universities.

Volunteering Leads to Networking and Leadership Roles

One of the exciting opportunities in college and universities is volunteering. When a student is an accounting major in college or at a university, taking their knowledge from the classroom to the field is exciting. Volunteering with organizations one is familiar with or the first introduction from a friend begins new networking opportunities. Accounting firms support volunteering for their employees. College and university students who focus their time towards internships at an accounting firm open doors for further networking. Uniting women and community service is empowering when accounting firms strategically targets their volunteer programs. Targeted volunteering provides women accountants with networking and the opportunity to develop better networking skills to advance to leadership and partner opportunities in their accounting firms. This dynamic design aligns women's since of purpose with professional goals. The dynamic provides a frame of reference between loyalty and career. Women enjoy the opportunities to make a difference while working with colleagues and community service.

Volunteering expands careers when women are involved with not-for-profits and community based organizations outside of their immediate career expertise. Accounting firms with successful community service programs are successful in employee investment. Accounting Move Project (2012) commented that 71% of firms offer leadership training through volunteering in community service, 64% of firms offer leadership training through volunteer business board positions, 79% offer leadership training through not-for-profit volunteer board positions, and 36% offer organization marketing connected to sponsorship or support of entrepreneurs. When accounting firms include paid time to volunteer in community services within their corporate social responsibility (CSR), women make fewer hard choices between their personal and professional decisions. In addition, women who volunteer their time and talent to a finance committee in an organization, find themselves working in smaller roles, such as, marketing and team leadership building with young adults.

This presents opportunities to expand in generational diversity and operational roles unlike accounting responsibilities. One develops deeper talents in different areas other than the initial career choice. Volunteering is giving without expecting anything in return. Forbes Insight (2011) commented that companies with philanthropy and community service set three top business goals: 66% of the companies believe in improving employee motivation, 64% of companies believe in increasing and improving employee skills and leadership, and 59% of the companies believe in the goal of differentiating one's own company from their competitors.

Income tax assistance programs in the local area are good organizations to contact for volunteering to help. Volunteering is not always about enhancing your profile. One may not have knowledge on taxes, but volunteering can offer a training opportunity to help career aspirations. Volunteering opens many doors to opportunities that expand one's knowledge and skills. Helping charitable organizations includes volunteering with gifting programs, estate planning, and direct funding as well (Forbes, 2013).

Volunteering Female Students

One of the highest motivators of students volunteering is the opportunity to gain work-related experience, new skills, and qualifications that help further their education and career endeavors. A volunteer student mentors with a professional woman in accounting that supports the self-confidence of learning within the student. Experiences learned from an Inquiry-based learning classroom explored and shared with a mentor is an exciting experience.

A leadership role for young college students is volunteering for tutoring, teaching, and mentoring youth. According to Date, Kramer, Dietz, and Grimm (2006), 30.2% female college students volunteer for educational or youth organizations. Within the hospital or other health-related organizations, 64.5%, volunteers are female college students (Date et al., 2006).

Conclusion

Preparing students for real-life career sustainability in leadership involves more than providing students with content related to framework themes. Inverting the classroom is reversing professor-guided classrooms to student-driven classrooms (Inquiry-based learning). The Inquiry-based learning model empowers students to ask questions, engage in-group settings, problem solving to stimulate the mind. The thinking process begins with reflective thinking then moves to critical thinking and produces decisions that support refractive thinking. An Inquiry-based learning classroom environment supports refractive thinking by giving students an actual voice in the classroom to explore beyond traditional boundaries. Teaching using lecture in accounting courses applies the analytical and theory techniques, not the practical application experience. Without refractive thinking, students fail to continue critical thinking and problem solving.

Accounting is more than numbers. Women's advancing into higher-level leadership is increasing with the increase of women business entrepreneurs. This is a competitive advantage for women in accounting. The change in the accounting profession accommodates flexible arrangements making accounting attractive to the younger generation. Accounting classrooms in colleges and universities is the environment for developing leadership skills. The Inquiry-based learning classroom gives access to real world professor experiences and the outcomes of the experiences.

College and university students who focus their time towards internships at an accounting firm open doors for further networking. Uniting women and community service is empowering when accounting firms strategically targets their volunteer programs. Targeted volunteering provides women accountants with networking and the opportunity to develop better networking skills to advance to leadership and partner opportunities in their accounting firms. This dynamic design aligns women's since of purpose with professional goals. The dynamic provides a frame of reference between loyalty and career. Women enjoy the opportunities to make a difference while working with colleagues and community service accommodates generation diversity.

THOUGHTS FROM THE ACADEMIC ENTREPRENEUR

The problem to be solved:
- Creating refractive thinking in the classroom to inspire accounting leadership in women.

The goals:
- Classroom influences refractive thinking preparing students for real-life career sustainability in accounting and leadership roles.
- Classroom influences leadership styles between men and women students in an Inquiry-based learning flexible environment (student-driven environment).

The questions to ask:
- Should the take away from a classroom be directed towards the business applications for networking, leadership training, and volunteering in accounting for students?
- Why are there fewer women partners in accounting firms?
- Is target volunteering a better method for women to align their since of purpose and professional goals?

Today's Business Application:
- Introducing Inquiry-based learning into the classroom stimulates reflective thinking, critical thinking, and refractive thinking to apply to internships and volunteering.
- Developing leadership styles, communications, team focus, problem solving to apply to internships.
- Volunteering leads to networking and leadership roles by uniting women and community service through accounting firms that strategically target their volunteer programs within their corporate social responsibility (CSR) area.

- Empowering students to become involved in internship programs in accounting firms and volunteering programs to develop networking skills and train in leadership.

REFERENCES

Accounting Move Project Executive Report. (2012). *Building careers and communities: How strategic community service advances women in public accounting.* Retrieved from http://www.mossadams.com/mossadams/media/Documents/About/Forum_W/MOVE-2012-Report.pdf

American Institute of Certified Public Accountants (AICPA). (2016). *The most important issues for women in the accounting profession.* Retrieved from http://www.aicpa.org/interestareas/youngcpanetwork/resources/career/pages/themostimportantissuesforwomenintheaccountingprofession.aspx

American Institute of Certified Public Accountants (AICPA). (2015). *2015 trends in the supply of accounting graduates and the demand for public accounting recruits.* Retrieved from http://www.aicpa.org/InterestAreas/AccountingEducation/NewsAndPublications/DownloadableDocuments/2015-TrendsReport.pdf

Catalyst. (2016). *Quick take: Women in accounting.* Retrieved from http://www.catalyst.org/knowledge/women-accounting

Colley, B., Bilics, A., & Lerch, C. (2012) Reflection: a key component to thinking critically. *The Canadian Journal for the Scholarship of Teaching and Learning, 3*(1), 1–9. http://dx.doi.org/o10.5206/cjsotl-rcacea.2o012.1.2

Date, L., Cramer, K., Dietz, N., & Grimm, R. (2006). *College students helping America.* Retrieved from http://www.nationalservice.gov/pdf/06_1016_RPD_college_full.pdf

El-Ramly, Y. (2013). Women's initiatives: A strategic advantage. *Journal of Accountancy.* Retrieved from http://www.journalofaccountancy.com/issues/2013/sep/20137820.html

Forbes. (2013). *six volunteer opportunities for finance professionals.* Retrieved from http://www.forbes.com/sites/investopedia/2013/06/26/6-volunteer-opportunities-for-finance-professionals/

Forbes Insight. (2011). *Corporate philanthropy the new paradigm: Volunteerism. Competence. Results.* Retrieved from http://www.forbes.com/forbesinsights/philanthropy_csr_2011/index.htm

Jacobs, P., & Schain, L. (2009). Professional women: the continuing struggle for acceptance and equality. *Journal of Academic and Business Ethics, 1*, 98–111. Retrieved from http//www.aabri.com/manuscripts/08056.pdf

Kitaoka, H. (2011). Teaching methods that help economics students to be effective problem solvers. *Social Science Research Network.* http://dx.doi.orgg/10.2139/ssrn.1951095

Limbach, B., Duron, R., & Waugh, W. (2008). Become a better teacher: Five steps in the direction of critical thinking. *Research in Higher Education Journal, 1*, 1–13. Retrieved from http://aabri.com/manuscripts/08059.pdf

Pfeffer, J., & Fong, C.T. (2002). The end of business schools? Less success than meets the eye. *Academy of Management Learning & Education, 1*(1). http//dx.doi.org/10.5465/amle.2002.7373679

Prayitno, A., Subanji, & Muksar, M. (2016). Refractive thinking with dual strategy in solving mathematics problem. *Journal of Research & Method in Education, 6*(3), 49–56. doi:10.79790/7388-0603034956

Thompson, F., & Washington, H. (2015). Critical thinking skills and teaching accounting: A comparative study. *Journal of Finance and Accountancy, 19*, 1–8.

Zwart, C. (2014). *How women leaders create the future.* Retrieved from https://www.ifac.org/global-knowledge-gateway/

About the Author ...

Dr. Michelle L. Boese resides in the historical Conifer, nestled in the Colorado Rocky Mountains west of Denver. She holds several accredited degrees; a Bachelor of Science (BS) in Accounting from Colorado Technical University (CTU), Colorado Springs, Colorado; a Master of Business Administration (MBA) in Accounting from CTU; and a Doctorate of Business Administration (DBA) in Accounting from Argosy University.

Dr. Michelle is an Assistant Professor at CTU and teaches accounting online and ground campuses. She enjoys the interaction with students, striving to provide a pathway to academic excellence within the classroom. She is a member of the National Society of Collegiate Scholars. She is a Subject Matter Expert (SME) creating course designs in the graduate and undergraduate online accounting curriculum for CTU.

Dr. Michelle founded her firm, MSB & Associates, LLC, in 1985. She presently serves on the Board of Directors for the Guardians of Six Pages as the Director of Strategic Planning and volunteers as the Accounting Chair for the American Cancer Society. She served as the past Director in 2002 for the Elizabeth Bowen Children's Home.

To reach Dr. Michelle L. Boese for information on consulting or doctoral coaching, please e-mail: mboese9@gmail.com

6

The Power of Promoting Women in Leadership through Mentoring and Networking

Dr. Patricia A. Champion & Dr. Linda J. Gutsch

The rationale to promote mentoring and networking collaboration is complex, yet straightforward, as its merits are many regarding promoting power for women in leadership. Many would agree that mentoring is a relationship between two people for professional and personal development, often career oriented, with an experienced person guiding the protégé (Kaur, 2015). Access to a strong network of contacts with which women can interact and gain support for their work and activities promotes the cause for which they are working, as well as helps to move an entire organization forward. By mentoring women for successful leadership roles, a conduit through which organizations can develop and promote some of their most valuable human resources can be realized. When that potential is fully realized, mentoring can contribute meaningfully to an organization's longevity and growth (Mertz, Welch, & Henderson, 1990). Refractive thinking encourages the reader to process and consider what it means to be a mentor, the mentor / protégé relationship, and its purpose. With consideration to the power of mentoring women in leadership, a short compilation of some mentoring strategies, programs, and mentoring support systems will be considered through the lens of educational leadership, and Science, Technology, Engineering, and Math (STEM).

The Power of Promoting Women in Leadership through Mentoring and Networking

> "A mentor is someone who allows you to see the hope inside yourself. A mentor is someone who allows you to know that no matter how dark the night, in the morning joy will come. A mentor is someone who allows you to see the higher part of yourself when sometimes it becomes hidden from your own view."
>
> —Oprah Winfrey

When King Odysseus of Ithaca went to fight in the Trojan War, he left his young son, Telemachus, under the care of Mentor, a teacher and caretaker, overseeing Odysseus' home and family while he was away. From the Greek legend, the term *mentor* has come to mean a teacher, friend, trusted advisor, and knowledgeable guide. Throughout history many examples of successful mentorships exist; Socrates and Plato, Hayden and Beethoven, Freud and Jung, Gandhi and Dr. Martin Luther King, Jr., Bing Crosby and Frank Sinatra, Walter Cronkite and Dan Rather, and the list goes on. This list mirrors research on the topic of mentoring, as the majority of both mentors and mentees are men. Women can benefit from the advantages of mentoring and networking.

Power of Mentoring

Mentoring is a relationship between two people for professional and personal development, often career oriented, with the experienced person guiding the novice. Mentoring is the informal transmission of knowledge, social capital, and the psychosocial support that is most relevant to work, career or professional advancement (Kaur, 2015). In a study about traditional mentoring in business, five techniques were labeled as common strategies that can be most effective. The first three strategies include a) accompanying—when the mentor shows caring commitment by taking part in the learning process along with the learner, b) sowing—by preparing the mentee ahead of time for new learning that may require advance scaffolding, and c) catalyzing—when the mentor plunges the mentee into a new learning situation to help change and re-order their thinking. The final two strategies help complete the mentoring model; d) showing—when the mentor demonstrates by example, and e) harvesting—by asking reflective questions to help the mentee deepen their new levels of understanding and learning (Kaur, 2015). Through skillful mentoring, the mentee will begin to assume the leadership traits that have been honed, and both the individual and the business benefit from this leadership growth model of mentoring.

Women's ways of knowing and learning often are based on building relationships both personally and professionally in the way they approach their careers (Belencky, 1986). Mentoring, in the more traditional sense, includes definition as hierarchical, women find more success in relational mentoring in which reciprocal partnerships are formed to benefit both the mentee and mentor. In this concept of reciprocal learning, both the mentor and mentee must be receptive to new insights and perspectives. Personal and shared reflections are important to deriving the most benefit from this model.

Psychosocial mentoring (friendship, acceptance, and support) is not often as valued as career mentoring (coaching for job strategizing, organizational mobility, and decision-making) for women, a balance of the two proves to be successful. In a new theory about relational mentoring, called *protégé' empowerment,* involves a relationship basis in which perception of developmental meaning, relational effects, interpersonal competence and self-determination all come into play. These elements promote high quality reciprocal interactions that benefit both protégés and the organization (Fullick-Jaeglia, 2015).

The benefits of mentoring are numerous, and in educational settings they play a critical role in the development of aspiring school leaders. Providing the opportunity to share, reflect and participate in professional development, offers both veteran educators and beginning, aspiring leaders the opportunity to collaborate and gain new perspectives on the challenges of educational leadership. Findings from research indicated that the mentoring relationships can have a positive influence on the leadership development of both the mentor and mentee through challenging each other's philosophies and beliefs (Clayton, Sanzo, & Myran, 2013), as well as dialoguing to explore and try new approaches and strategies. Implications and recommendations from individuals involved in educational mentoring models indicate that aspiring leaders need more time to engage in authentic leadership practices, more opportunities to engage in real-time school projects, and that both mentors and mentees need training to know what to expect and how best to take advantage to maximize the learning potential on both sides in the mentoring relationship (Clayton et al., 2013). To meet these goals, strategic visioning and planning must be developed and implemented.

With this research in the effects that mentoring can have, women continue to be under represented in upper management and in positions of power and authority. Women in the United States constitute 50.8% of the population; earn nearly 60% of undergraduate degrees, 60% of master's degrees, 47% of all law degrees, and 48% of all medical degrees (Warner, 2014). They earn more than 44% of master's degrees in business and management including 37% of the MBA's. Women are 47% of the U.S. labor force and 59% of the college-educated entry-level workforce. Despite these statistics, they hold 52% of all professional-level jobs, yet only 14.6% of executive officers, 8.1% of top earners and 4.6% of Fortune 500 Chief Executive Officers (CEOs). Women fall significantly behind men in leadership positions within the United States (Warner, 2014).

Realizing that efforts need to be made to support women in career development, many organizations adopt formal mentoring programs for women, with the goal of addressing gender differences in career advancement (Dworkin, Kwolek-Foll, Mauer, & Schipani, 2009). Women who are mentored are more likely to achieve promotions in their careers, higher salaries, superior compensation packages, increased career and organizational commitment, and an improved work and life balance (Leek, Elliott, & Rockwell, 2012). Mentoring for women has proven to be invaluable in providing guidance, how to gain insights, seize power, understand organizational politics, obtain useful feedback and gain access to the inner workings and resources of the organizations where they work (Leek et al., 2012).

Mentoring is most effective when women are mentored by other women, who can act as role models, who have experienced life *in the trenches,* and who can share the opportunities and challenges that may arise (Johnson, 2011). Women tend to be more at ease and can mirror *female behaviors* of women mentors, more so than the *masculine behaviors* of a male mentor. Women who display stronger, more dominant approaches, such as those exemplified by men in leadership, are often referred to as too aggressive or assertive, not understanding the *corporate structure pecking order* (Holmes, 2005). While acquiring a female leader as a mentor would benefit aspiring women leaders, as statistics prove, not enough women are available in top leadership positions to serve as mentors. The unfortunate side to this dilemma is that more men serve in senior management and C-suite settings, than women; thus, fewer women mentors are available.

In a study compiled by The Wall Street Journal with top women executives, mentoring was found to be important to these women on their career paths to top leadership positions (Bussey, 2012).

Although the top leadership is predominantly male, one woman noted that she had many male mentors, but the men did not know it because she picked their brains as often as possible. Managers at Google, Inc. said they had to encourage women to apply for management positions because by the time these potential hires did apply, they had to be prodded, and more than likely they had been ready for the leadership role a year earlier. Women need to be risk-takers and take advantage of opportunities rather than waiting to be asked and to pursue new skills relentlessly (Bussey, 2012). The power of promoting women in leadership through mentoring is strengthened when women have advocates who support and encourage them to pursue leadership opportunities.

Power of Networking

Women seeking advanced leadership careers benefit from mentors and advocates who support and encourage them, and who help them in acquiring the power of a well-connected network. Social research indicates what women have experienced; mentoring teamed with networking can help them reach the highest positions of leadership in their respective businesses. Developing a strong network of contacts with which women can interact and gain support for the work and activities they are engaged in, promotes the cause for which they are working on, and helps move the entire organization forward. An individual's network can be powerful and can provide professional guidance, experience, contacts, and can help advance the careers of those who can skillfully use and manage their network. When a woman can build a network to help promote herself and her causes, the larger and more diverse the network, the more benefit it will add (Choi & Miller, 2012).

Networking among women provides the opportunity to share ideas, problem solve together, exchange business contacts and resources, along with the possibility of making valuable connections to aid each other in career advancement or promotions. One of the most important aspects of networking is building relationships. Women connect with others through friendship, common interests, family ties, hobbies, and work related interests, just to name a few. A most important and valuable aspect of networking for women is in building lasting relationships (Eagly & Carli, 2009). Where men may trade business cards or share a round of golf, for women who network, it is not just about business, it is about life. Women tend to reach out with advice or a helping hand. When another woman asks for help, if the person she asks does not know, she can tap into her own network and find a solution. The power of networking provides professional gain and personal relationships (Rappaport, 2015).

With a strong network, perhaps women can shift the balance of power that has stood as a barrier for too many years. Women stood by believing that they would rise through the ranks because of the hard work they exhibited, only to watch a man with less seniority be promoted over women who were more qualified but did not obtain the job because the man was better connected to the C-suite peer group. This type of networking needs to become second nature to women, so that they will become self-promoters who know how to advocate for themselves and have a strong network who can help leverage support for career growth and success (Ragins, 1996).

Lisa Lambert, Vice-President of Intel Capital, interviewed three women in leadership: Wendy Becham, Managing Principal with the Leadership and Talent Consulting Practice of Korn Ferry; Melissa Daimler, head of global learning and organizational development at Twitter; and Pat Wadors, Senior Vice President of Global Talent Development at LinkedIn. Ms. Lambert asked for their advice to help promote the power of women in leadership. They offered five tips: a) integrate instead of balance, b) have a goal, c) do your homework, d) arrive at the point, and e) use all your networks (Lambert, 2015). Leadership opportunities are there, and it is up to women to use the mentors and develop the networks to take them where their aspirations lead.

Power of Mentoring Women in Educational Leadership

Regarding the literature available for mentoring women to positions of power in educational leadership, mentoring is for the most part widely defined, infrequently/ineffectively used, is not especially visible (Gardiner, Grogan, & Enomoto, 1999; Mertz, 2004; Wasburn, 2007), and usually impacts equity issues rather than access in educational fields (Gupton & Slick, 1998). In particular, women being mentored into educational leadership roles within public school systems have traditionally been a part of an androcentric culture of educational administration (Gardiner et al., 1999; Gardiner, Enomoto, & Grogan, 2000; Mertz, Welch, & Henderson, 1990; Mertz, 2004). Women aspiring to administrative leadership positions within school systems often experience conflicts concerning the unwritten rules they often know nothing about within this school system culture, not the least of which includes the relationship between the mentor / protégé, including personal issues such as raising families, attending night school, gender expectations / stereotypes, and determining the best timing for a possible career/ leadership role advancement (Gardiner et al., 1999). In this regard, the power of mentoring can help shape a woman's educational leadership effectiveness because mentoring can play a critical role to determine how women can successfully combine their professional and personal lives into successful careers (Gardiner et al., 1999).

To achieve success as a female educational leader with the attendant situations associated with women seeking leadership roles, varying methods and strategies exist to successfully mentor and subsequently promote educational female leaders. One, for example, is the *Administrative Leadership Academy* (ALA) with its

Entry Year Program component developed for early career principals is an effort to proactively address common challenges and reduce stress associated with more traditional, top-down mentor / protégé relationships. In ALA's program, mentors are trained to know when to instruct, to coach or facilitate indicative of a more collaborative, teamwork-oriented approach to mentoring (Peters, 2010). Early-career female principals were viewed within the context of the ALA's approach deconstructing the notion of traditional one-on-one, hierarchical relationships resulting in a successful, collaborative team-oriented mentoring concept (Peters, 2010). "By reframing traditional notions of mentoring, these relationships can be more broadly defined such that mentoring roles are performed by several people simultaneously" (Peters, 2010, p. 126). The idea that one person can assume more than one role in the mentor/protégé relationship (Gardiner et al., 2000) is proactively incorporated into the ALA's framework and the traditional mentor/protégé relationship being neutralized allows the mentor to serve as a mutual learner to assist the female protégé through various challenges, while encouraging the development of the female protégé's leadership style (Gardiner et al., 2000; Peters, 2010).

Wasburn (2007) submitted a networking (peer) mentoring, non-hierarchical model whereby female faculty (from a case study of universities) utilized a community of participants (more than two) as mentors for their protégés, echoing the previous collaborative team-oriented mentoring concept (Gardiner et al., 2000; Peters, 2010). Research suggested this networking mentoring collaboration model to be more flexible, less intense (regarding compatibility) over periods of time than the traditional one-on-one model. Networking mentoring collaboration empowered participants because it encouraged a range of opinions, advice, perspectives, and social support, all in an environment that women typically prosper and thrive in, suggesting that peer networking collaboration can be particularly useful regarding the power of mentoring women seeking career advancement in higher education faculties (Wasburn, 2007).

Regarding whether gender or equity differences influence the effectiveness of one-on-one mentor / protégé relationships for women in educational leadership, preliminary data (Schneider, 1991), indicated that men are still needed in the mentoring relationship, due in large part to the notion that mentoring men's career goals differs significantly with similar women's career aspirations. For example, when male protégés achieve their career objectives, or not, they often move on to another mentor or break from the relationship (Schneider, 1991). For some women, men continue to be needed in the traditional mentor role because women more times than not, find themselves overwhelmed with many responsibilities, and as a result, will continue (when possible) with their mentor (male or female) through all stages of their career development to help balance personal and professional responsibilities, including asking more questions related to readiness and skill development than male protégés (Schneider, 1991).

Power of Mentoring Women in Science, Technology, Engineering & Math

Science, Technology, Engineering, and Math (STEM) fields often lack women in leadership positions, who face a spectrum of barriers as women faculty in STEM, those working toward degree completion, or those who do make it into their respective STEM field, which leaves a dearth of women experiencing leadership power in STEM (Dawson, Bernstein, & Bekki, 2015). As a result, women are leaving STEM fields, not necessarily because of a deficit in academic preparation, ability, or talent per se (Seymour, 1995; Sonnert & Holton, 1995), but rather from a loss in confidence and support networks often triggered by a range of experiences along the STEM pathway (Dawson et al., 2015). As a result, women continue to be underrepresented in STEM, and especially in STEM leadership and faculty positions (Dawson et al., 2015; Gorman, Durmowicz, Roskes, & Slattery, 2010). This situation exists initially from women experiencing limited access to advisors and mentors "who can provide the psychosocial aspects of mentoring that have been shown to bolster success and persistence, buffer discouragement, and attenuate decisions to leave science" (Dawson et al., 2015, p. 59), followed by a lack of networking collaboration leading to issues regarding self-assurance in a field dominated by men both in and out of school (Dawson et al., 2015).

To remediate this situation for example, The Ohio State University initiated peer mentoring circles for women STEM faculty members (Thomas, Bystydzienski, & Desai, 2015). Because STEM male faculty outnumber STEM female faculty, chief among the central questions for their research was to see if the circles would contribute to retention of women faculty members, followed by examining how the peer mentoring circles would engage women faculty facilitated meetings serving as mentors for each other, providing mutual support, and helping to bring about a change in culture aimed at improvements for women STEM faculty in higher education (Thomas et al., 2015). The primary suggestions regarding improvements included a need for better session organization, modifying sessions to a needs-based framework while incorporating individual needs assessments to determine individual goals (Thomas et al., 2015).

For women STEM students and graduate students at Syracuse University the Women in Science and Engineering (WiSE) and the WiSE Future Professionals Program (WiSE-FPP) collaborated with the Graduate School and Colleges of Engineering and Computer Science and Arts and Sciences to create a peer support network for women graduate students in science and engineering

(Bhatia & Amati, 2010). The effect of this collaboration provided the women the academic and technical skill development for leadership roles, but of central importance, the necessary support networks with peers. Because of the inherent isolation women in STEM experience, opportunities for students to develop peer support systems to be able to listen and learn from other STEM graduate women was central to the WiSE-FPP framework, as it allowed a venue to build relationships, which would later transcend to successful STEM leaders (Bhatia et al., 2010).

Another highly effective service that can provide the psychosocial benefits of mentoring women in STEM is an approach to mentoring coined *Career*WiSE sponsored by Arizona State University project, supported by the National Science Foundation (Dawson et al., 2015).

> The *Career*WiSE program of psychological education provides instruction, practice, and vicarious role models, customized for women in STEM fields, in personal and interpersonal skills for overcoming discouragers, managing barriers, and expanding supports to fulfill personal and professional ambitions. The framework extends the problem-solving method that scientists and engineers use for technical problems to the personal and interpersonal issues associated with advancement in academic arenas. (Dawson et al., 2015, p. 57)

The website also showcased role models and training clips, including an interactive, multimedia simulation with live actors to supplement curriculum regarding a specific set of communication skills designed to "lessen the risks associated with a range of barriers and unwelcoming environments encountered by women in STEM . . . [and that] women in STEM will obtain the skills, resources, and encouragement they need to combat discouragement and to persist in STEM education, occupations, and careers" (Dawson et al., 2015, p. 59).

Finally and of special note, in the School of the Sciences (SOS) at Stevenson University an anomaly exists, as 71% of the full-time STEM faculty members are female and 100% of the academic leadership in STEM is provided by women (Gorman et al., 2010). The staff ratios set the university apart with respect to other universities around the country with four types of mentoring relationships within the School of the Sciences: "mentoring leaders, mentoring faculty, mentoring students, and mentoring others outside the University" (Gorman et al., 2010, p. 4) affecting how students view STEM women in leadership because it actively demonstrates a leadership model that works. Unique within these mentoring relationships the university has implemented a web infrastructure to support its STEM faculty and students (Gorman et al., 2010).

> Together with an informed, innovative approach to curriculum reform, synergistic leadership and management strategies have allowed the School of the Sciences at SU to do more with less in STEM education. Fundamental to this success has been the evolution of a mentoring web within the STEM academic unit, which is led entirely by women . . . The nature of the mentoring is tailored to the position of the participants involved, but in each case the mentoring contributes to professional growth and development. The emphasis on mentoring has contributed to an increased sense of community and collegiality in the SOS and has enabled the School of the Sciences to make rapid progress in STEM curricular reform and program improvement. (Gorman et al., 2010, p. 1)

In a practical application sense, the mentoring framework employed in the School of the Sciences at Stevenson University promotes an ideal solution regarding the school's support for promoting the power of mentoring women and future leadership role possibilities for these women, as the mentoring web is there to catch STEM students seeking its council.

Conclusion

Refractive thinkers might consider the value of mentoring and networking with consideration to the multi-dimensional facets involved in the power of being an effectual mentor. Through discussions of hierarchal mentor experiences related to issues and conflicts unique to women, as well as the many benefits of promoting mentoring and networking collaboration, all have played a critical role regarding the importance of promoting women in leadership in various settings with regard to cultural changes and support for aspiring female leaders. From this we have demonstrated how important mentoring is for women, and how having access to willing, strong advocates is a beginning for promoting women in leadership through mentoring and networking infrastructures that can support our most valuable potential female leaders. Additionally, this chapter also delineated how mentoring, in the more traditional sense defined as hierarchical, has resulted with women experiencing conflicts as they seem to have found more success in relational mentoring support systems where reciprocal partnerships are formed to benefit both the protégé and mentor.

While the lack of female role models remains a barrier for women advancing in engineering careers, and other educational careers, our research suggests that peer support networks have also contributed to the academic and career success for women in these fields. Through skillful mentoring, and peer support networking collaboration, female protégés can develop important leadership traits to assume leadership roles, benefitting both the individual and the organization. Whether mentoring in a STEM field, higher education, school district, or in a corporate setting, these entities can benefit from comprehensive leadership mentoring models for promoting women to positions of leadership.

Although several programs, strategies, and resources proved

successful regarding staying power and resilience for women in seeking leadership positions, whether it be in educational leadership, or Science, Technology, Engineering, and Math (STEM) fields, refractive thinkers realize there remains much more to study and know about the importance of developing valuable mentoring programs to support a new generation of different leaders; more female than male, more ethnically minority than majority. This chapter included insight into some of those challenges, as well as learning about some successful mentoring programs, resources and peer networking collaboration models.

THOUGHTS FROM THE ACADEMIC ENTREPRENEUR

The problem to be solved:

- Developing, promoting, networking and mentoring women in leadership positions.

The goals:

- Understanding the power of mentoring and networking processes for women leading to leadership roles, positions and careers.

The questions to ask:

- What is effectual mentoring?
- Networking vs mentoring: what is the difference and effectiveness of each?
- What are some of the most effective mentoring, role modeling, networking strategies and programs for promoting the power of women?

Today's Business Application:

- Effective mentors can help women achieve leadership positions, career advancement, increased career and organizational commitment, gain understandings of organizational politics, and become reflective, focused leaders.

- Leadership preparation through the lens of mentoring and networking is a step to help women leap beyond the glass ceiling.

- Continuous exploration and making use of networking and mentoring processes, strategies and programs can influence and result in leadership roles and careers for women.

REFERENCES

Belenky, M. F., Clinchy, B. M., Goldberger, N. R., & Tarule, J. M. (1996). *Women's ways of knowing*. New York, NY: Basic Books.

Bhatia, S., & Amati, J. (2010, October). If these women can do it, I can do it, too: Building women engineering leaders through graduate peer mentoring. *Leadership Management in Engineering, 10*(4), 174–184. Retrieved from http://ascelibrary.org/doi/pdf/10.1061/%28ASCE%29LM.1943-5630.0000081

Bussey, J. (2012, May 18). How women can get ahead: Advice from female CEO's. *Wall Street Journal*. Retrieved from http://www.wsj.com/articles/SB10001424052702303879604577410520511235252

Choi, S., & Miller, R. (2012). Mentoring, networking and leadership. *Laryngoscope, 122*. doi:10.1002/lary.23598

Clayton, J. K., Myrian, S., & Sanzo, K. L. (2013). Understanding mentoring in leadership development: Perspectives of district administrators and aspiring leaders. *Journal of Research on Leadership Education, 8*(1), 7–96. doi:10.1177/1942775112464959

Dawson, A. E., Bernstein, B. L., & Bekki, J. M. (2015, Fall). Providing the psychosocial benefits of mentoring to women in STEM: *Career*WiSE as an online solution. *New Directions for Higher Education*, (171), 53–62. Retrieved from http://onlinelibrary.wiley.com/doi/10.1002/he.20142/full

Dworkin, T., Kwolek-Foll, A., Mauer, V. G., & Schipani, C. (2009). Pathways for women to obtain positions of organization leadership: The significance of mentoring and networking, 16(1), 89–136. *Duke Journal of Gender Law & Policy.* Retrieved from http://scholarship.law.duke.edu/djglp/vol16/iss1/3/

Eagly, A. H., & Carli, L. L. (2009, September). Navigating the labyrinth: For women, the glass ceiling has been replaced by complex and circuitous obstacles to high-level leadership roles. *The School Administrator, 66*(8). Retrieved from http://www.aasa.org/SchoolAdministratorArticle.aspx?id=5662

Fullick-Jaeglia, J. M., Verbos, A. K., Wiese, C. W. (2015, December). Relational mentoring episodes as a catalyst for empowering protégés: A conceptual model. *Human Resource Development Review, 14,* 486–508. doi:10.1177/1534484315610730

Gardiner, M. E., Grogan, M., & Enomoto, E. (1999). *Women's conflicts as they are mentored into educational leadership in public schools.* Retrieved from http://files.eric.ed.gov/fulltext/ED460949.pdf

Gardiner, M. E., Enomoto, E., & Grogan, M. (2000). *Coloring outside the lines: Mentoring women into school leadership.* New York, NY: State University of New York Press.

Gorman, S. T., Durmowicz, M. C., Roskes, E. M., & Slattery, S. P. (2010). Women in the academy: Female leadership in STEM education and the evolution of a mentoring web. *Forum on Public Policy, Online, 2010*(2). Retrieved from http://files.eric.ed.gov/fulltext/EJ903573.pdf

Gupton, S. L., & Slick, G. A. (1998). Highly successful women administrators: The inside stories of how they got there. *National Association of Secondary School Principals. NASSP Bulletin, 82*(594), 120–121. Retrieved from http://bul.sagepub.com/content/82/594/120.extract#

Holmes, J. (2005). Leadership talk: How do leaders 'do mentoring', and is gender relevant? *Journal of Pragmatics, 37,* 1779–1800. Retrieved from http://anothersample.net/leadership-talk-how-do-leaders-do-mentoring-and-is-gender-relevant

Johnson, D. (2011). Mentoring and support systems: Keys to leadership. *Advancing Women in Leadership, 31*(1), 40–44. Retrieved from http://awljournal.org/Vol31_2011/Johnson_final6_2_17.pdf

Kaur, J. (2015). Enhancing leadership competencies through mentoring process. *International Journal of Management Research and Reviews, 5*(4), 265–269. Retrieved from http://ijmrr.com/admin/upload_data/journal_Dr%20Jaideep%20Kaur%20%205apr15mrr.pdf

Lambert, L. (2015). 5 networking tips from three great women. *Upward Women.* Retrieved from http://www.upwardwomen.org/moveup/5-networking-tips/

Leck, J. D., Elliott, C., & Rockwell, B. (2012). E-mentoring women: Lessons learned from a pilot program. *Journal of Diversity Management (Online), 7*(2), 83. Retrieved from http://www.cluteinstitute.com/ojs/index.php/JDM/article/view/7476/7542

Mertz, N., Welch, O., & Henderson, J. (1990). Executive mentoring: Myths, issues, and strategies. Retrieved from http://files.eric.ed.gov/fulltext/ED323635.pdf

Mertz, N. T. (2004). What's a mentor anyway? *Educational Administration Quarterly, 40,* 541–560. doi:10.1177/0013161X04267110

Peters, A. (2010). Elements of successful mentoring of a female school leader. *Leadership and Policy in Schools, 9*(1), 108–129. doi:10.1080/15700760903026755

Ragins, B. R. (2011). Relational mentoring: A positive approach to mentoring at work. In K. Cameron & G. Spreitzer (Eds.), *The Oxford handbook of positive organizational scholarship,* (pp. 519–536). New York, NY: Oxford University Press. Retrieved from http://ellenensher.com/wp-content/uploads/2013/06/Ragins-2012-Relational-Mentoring-Chapter-Handbook-of-POS.pdf

Rappaport, L. (2015, October 1). Networking isn't easy for women but it's crucial. *Wall Street Journal.* Retrieved from http://www.wsj.com/articles/networking-isnt-easy-for-women-but-it-is-crucial-1443600526

Seymour, E. (1995, October). The loss of women from science, mathematics, and engineering undergraduate majors: An explanatory account. *Science Education, 79,* 437–73. doi:10.1002/sce.3730790406

Schneider, A. M. (1991, November 23). *Mentoring women and minorities into positions of educational leadership: Gender differences and implications for mentoring.* Paper presentation at the annual meeting of the National Council of States on In-service Education, Houston, TX.

Sonnert, G., & Holton, G. J. (1995). *Who succeeds in science? The gender dimension.* New Brunswick, NJ: Rutgers University Press.

Thomas, N., Bystydzienski, J., & Desai, A. (2015). Changing institutional culture through peer mentoring of women STEM faculty. *Innovative Higher Education, 40*(2), 143–157. doi:10.1007/s10755-014-9300-9

Warner, J. (2015). The women's leadership gap: Women's leadership by the numbers. *Center for American Progress.* Retrieved from https://www.americanprogress.org/issues/women/report/2015/08/04/118743/the-womens-leadership-gap/

Wasburn, M. H. (2007, January). Mentoring women faculty: An instrumental case study of strategic collaboration. *Mentoring & Tutoring: Partnership in Learning, 15*(1), 57–72. doi:10.1080/13611260601037389

About the Authors...

A Coloradoan, Dr. Patricia (Trish) A. Champion holds several degrees including a Bachelor of Arts (BA) from the University of Northern Colorado; a Master of Arts (MA) in Curriculum and Instruction from the University of Northern Colorado; and a Doctorate of Education (Ed.D.) in Educational Leadership from the University of Phoenix School of Advanced Studies. She also holds state endorsements in Early Childhood and Gifted and Talented Education from the University of Northern Colorado.

Dr. Trish is a former teacher of gifted and talented education in Cherry Creek School District for more than 20 years. She is currently a university professor serving as adjunct assistant faculty online for the University of Iowa in the Belin-Blank International Center for Gifted Education and Talent Development.

Dr. Trish is an active member in Delta Kappa Gamma Sorority, American Association of University Women, and Pi Lambda Theta, an honor society for professional educators. Her doctoral study, *Equity vs Excellence: A Delphi study examining the future ramifications of NCLB on gifted education programs* provided her the opportunity to publish her study in *Kaleidoscope Magazine* (2008, June), a journal for educators of gifted and talented students.

To reach Dr. Patricia (Trish) A. Champion, please email: trchampion@comcast.net

Dr. Linda J. Gutsch, a Bachelor of Science (BS) in Elementary Education from Kansas State University, a Master of Arts (MA) in Curriculum and Instruction from the University of Denver, and a Doctor of Philosophy (PhD) in Educational Leadership and Policy Studies from the University of Denver. She holds endorsements as an elementary teacher and school administrator.

Dr. Linda is an Associate Faculty Member of the University of Phoenix, approved to teach courses in the Masters in Educational Administration Program and the School of Advanced Studies for the University of Phoenix, where she serves as a Dissertation Chair and committee member. In addition, Dr. Linda reviews and revises curriculum for the College of Education at University of Phoenix, and supervises student teachers.

Dr. Linda serves as an educational consultant in the areas of staff development and school improvement. She has served as a facilitator for Critical Friends Groups, and the Learning Network. She is a member of Phi Delta Kappa, an international association for professional educators. Her doctoral research, *A Study of Women Elementary School Principals Perceptions of Gender Issues,* provided her the opportunity to share her passion for women and leadership in education and gave her entry into teaching online with students from around the world.

To reach Dr. Linda J. Gutsch for information on consulting or doctoral coaching, please email: drljgutsch@yahoo.com

7
Women as Leaders

Dr. Denise Mayo Moore

The recent *Women in the Workplace* 2015, study by LeanIn.Org and McKinsey & Company, confirms that women remain underrepresented and face barriers when it comes to securing top leadership positions. The goal is of this chapter is to explore the characteristics of strong leaders and gender differences. One must consider the unique competencies required to overcome the gender bias and stereotypes that women encounter in the workplace. The point of this chapter is to unpack the implications of the statistical data gathered from the workplace, and to examine both the progress up to this point, and the many challenges that women still face even in today's supposedly more egalitarian era.

Women Leadership Worldwide

Globally, the United Nations (UN) prioritizes the inequality of women in both developed and developing nations. The UN Millennium Development Goals (UN, 2003) specifically addressed women-related issues, encouraging gender equality and the empowerment of women. Participation in the UN Division for the Advancement of Women (DAW) (UN, 2005) promotes equality with men across the world for sustainable development, peace and security, governance, and human rights.

According to UN data (2016), of the current 193 member states,

22% have female leadership. Highlights of global female leadership include, England, which has been under the leadership of Queen Elizabeth since 1952 and Denmark, under Queen Margrette's leadership since 1972. Within the past 50 years, India, Ireland, and Bangladesh all experienced female leadership in excess of 20 years. Women have led Germany, Liberia, Finland and Norway for over 11 years.

In many areas of the world, however, women continue to fight for the same human rights afforded to men. The UN maintains a Gender Inequality Index (GII), which ranks countries according to gender disparity. In 2013, the top five countries for the least gender inequality were: a) Slovenia, b) Switzerland, c) Germany, d) Sweden, and e) Denmark. While the bottom five countries with the most gender inequality were: 148, Mali; 149, Afghanistan; 150, Chad; 151, Niger, and 152, Yemen. The United States ranked 47th (UN, 2016). In the 21st century global market, Thompson (2015) pointed out the fragility of the gains made for women's rights and equality. Even with the support offered by the UN, some women leaders faced death. For example, Afghan women leaders continue to be assassinated in 2016. Pakistan native Malala Yousafzai, is the youngest Nobel Prize laureate, yet Malala was shot in an assassination attempt to silence her activism in education for girls (Thompson, 2015).

Women in the United States continue to seek equality in leadership positions with their male counterparts. Early U.S. women activists such as: Elizabeth Cady Stanton, Susan B. Anthony, Sojourner Truth, Lucretta Mott, Ida B. Wells, and countless others were instrumental in achieving rights for women, including, but not limited to the right to vote (McMillen, 2008). The right to vote was achieved for white women in 1920 (McMillen, 2008). African Americans did not attain the unrestricted right to vote until the Voting Rights Act passed in 1965 (McMillen, 2008). In 2016, statistics indicated women still struggle with equality. In America's large corporations, even though women comprise almost 50% of the workforce, they remain under-represented in top-level leadership positions (Bureau of Labor Statistics, 2015).

The Unique Historical Similarity of the United Nations and the United States

Overall, according to 2015 estimates by the UN, there are slightly more men than women in the world. However, these numbers do not include even distribution. In the United States, there are slightly more women than men, and women represent half of the U.S. labor force. Both the UN and the United States may have women leaders at the helm in 2016. The UN, as well as the United States, has a long history of women activists who fought for the equality of women.

One can certainly celebrate minor progress regarding the advancement of women in major companies in more recent years. A list of the top 500 American companies, aka Fortune 500, have a total of 21 females at the helm (Walker & Artiz, 2015). Women's nearly equal workforce representation is not mirrored in leadership positions. Women hold only 14.6% of executive officer positions in the Fortune 500; 16.9% of Fortune 500 board of director seats in 2013 were held by women, with little increase since 2013 (Walker & Aritz, 2015).

There are women who pierced the glass ceiling and are succeeding. For example, Indra Nooyi joined Pepsico in 1994 and was named President and Chief Financial Officer (CFO) in 2001. Mary Barra was elected Chairwomen of the GM Board of Directors on January 4, 2016. Jinni Rometty, became the President and Chief Executive Officer (CEO) of IBM in 2012. However, as Hillary Clinton, breaks the glass ceiling by likely winning the Democratic 2016 presidential nomination, she still faces skepticism. A recent Pew Research Center Report (2015) on women and leadership found that 37% of Americans believe the United States is just not ready to elect female leaders.

Women in the Workforce

According to the Bureau of Labor Statistics (BLS), in 2014, women accounted for 52% of all workers employed in management, professional, and related occupations. Specifically women accounted for more than half of all workers within several industry sectors: financial activities (53%); education and health services (75%); leisure and hospitality (51%); and other services (53%) (Bureau of Labor Statistics [BLS], 2014). Women remain substantially underrepresented (relative to their share of total employment) in agriculture (25%), mining (13%), construction (9%), manufacturing (29%), and transportation and utilities (23%) (BLS, 2014).

In terms of earnings, the gap between men and women still requires improvement. In 1979, women working full time earned 62% of what men earned (Walker & Artiz, 2015); in 2014, women's earnings were 83% of men's (Walker & Artiz, 2015). Women's educational strides also impacts the wage gap. Because of women's education, the wage gap margin between men and women was 41% in the 1970s and 21% in 2014 (Walker & Aritz, 2015). In the 1970s, women earned 59% of their male counterparts ("Women in the Workplace," 2015). In 2014, women earned 79% of what men were paid (BLS, 2015), however, women in leadership positions earned even less, 72.3% of their male colleagues (BLS, 2015). Overall, by age 65, women will have earned $430,000 less than men because of this wage gap ("Women in the Workplace," 2015). Compared to men, women do not have equal access to power, organizational leadership positions, or equal pay.

The examination of leadership advancement of women, based upon the lack of representation of women in executive leadership positions, is twofold. First, bias remains toward women continuing to perpetuate the problem and reinforces barriers to advancement. Second, current leadership maintains the status quo of limited interaction with women at executive levels. This result means that organizations will not realize the collaborative benefits of the female decision-making perspective. Research confirmed bias attitudes toward female leadership represents a large portion of both American and world views (McKinsey, 2015). The issues perpetuated by this concept create barriers to the advancement of women to senior leadership positions. Gender-related stereotypes and the expectations of and for women based upon stereotypes ensure that organizations must revisit cultural climate of inclusion practices. It remains a fact that to a large extent women do not hold positions that lead to upward management (Hunt, Layton, & Price, 2015).

Corporations must be held accountable to create equal access to opportunities for women who are prepared to assume senior positions. There is evidence that the corporate climate continues to change. In 2015, the major shareholder, Arjuna Capital requested eBay to publicly report the pay disparity between male and female employees and set goals to close the gap. Walmart continues to face the same type of public scrutiny. The disparity in wages is further highlighted by Patricia Arquette's call for wage equality during her 2015 Academy Awards acceptance speech "It's our time to have wage equality once and for all, and equal rights for women in the United States of America" (Rosen, 2015 p. 1). In his 2014 State of the Union address, President Obama declared "Women deserve equal pay for equal work. Gender inequality must be exposed and documented. Meaningful change cannot occur, if the incongruities are not measured and corrective action put in place" (Obama, 2014, p. 1).

Women Prepared to Lead

Educationally, women progressed over the past four decades. In developing countries, the average global university enrollment ratio in 1970 was 160 men per 100 women; today in 2016, it stands at 93 men per 100 women (Chanie, 2014). In the United States, women are almost 60% of the annual university graduates and more than 70% of 2012 high school valedictorians (Chanie, 2014). Women account for 60% of master's degrees and 52% of doctorates being awarded in the United States (Chanie, 2014). Statistically, worldwide women outnumber men in both university attendance and graduation.

Women prepare educationally for high-level leadership positions. Yet the parity in leadership positions remains distorted when regarding male counterparts. Women have been in the workforce for decades, but remain underrepresented in higher-level leadership positions. According to McKinsey (2015), 78% of top managers were men. Women are absent from school when it comes to Dean and higher-level administrative positions (McKinsey, 2015). Corporate boardrooms and CEO positions include approximately 10% female representation (McKinsey, 2015). Even though women represent almost 50% of the population, they only have 15% of Congressional representation (McKinsey, 2015).

Characteristics of Leaders

In 2016, corporate America slowly continues to move towards a more holistic management style which encompasses, soft as well as hard business skills. Rao (2014) suggested soft skills emphasize *how* one communicates, while hard skills emphasize *what* one communicates. In other words, soft skills are considered people skills such as; communication, self-management, networking, stress management, empathy, and other skills associated with Emotional Intelligence or EQ. Hard management skills are concrete and usually measurable. Performance reviews use hard skills to measure employee performance. Hard skills are associated with Intelligence quotient (IQ); these skills include math, finance, statistics, science, biology, and chemistry. There are several extensive studies regarding the strengths, skills, and characteristics of leadership in the workforce (Lopez-Zafra, 2012).

Hard as well as soft leadership skills are important; they can be learned and must be continuously improved. Zenger and Folkman (2012) studied 7,000 male and female leaders and concluded that female leaders excel in the categories of nurturing competencies such as developing others and building relationships, exhibiting integrity and engaging in self-development. Further conclusions were that women rated higher in 12 of the 16 competencies measured for outstanding leadership (Zenger & Folkman, 2012). Women received the highest scores in two competencies; taking initiative and driving for results (Zenger & Folkman, 2012). Men outscored women significantly on only one management competency in the study: the ability to develop a strategic perspective (Zenger & Folkman, 2012).

Contemporary research studies indicate women possess the education, experience and competencies making them exceeding prepared for leadership positions (Schuh et al., 2014). Indra Nooyi, is one of the most powerful women in the world. In a speech, Bhasin (2011) shared competencies and characteristics of Nooyi's leadership style. Nooyi philosophy is the Five C's.

Competency. Stand out from the pack and be a lifelong learner. Remain ahead and abreast in your field.

Courage and Confidence. Speak out. Establish your knowledge base and be confident in it as a leader.

Communication. Over-invest in written and oral communication. Leaders constantly have to motivate the troops.

Consistency. Remaining steady, reliable, and determined allows for credibility and a baseline to measure your successes and failures.

Compass. Integrity is critical in this job. (Bhasin, 2011, p. 3)

Pew's (2015) research study noted that men and women may believe female leaders are just as qualified as their male peers, but certain stigmas persist. Even in 2014, some 50% of women and 35% of men agree that many businesses are not ready to hire women for top executive positions (Pew, 2015). These findings are not congruent, however, with the research of Cook and Glass (2011). Cook and Glass found that corporate investors respond slightly more favorably to an announcement of a female than a male for top leadership positions. Pew found that 34% of the respondents believed that male executives are better than women at assuming risk. Zenger and Folkman (2012) found that as leaders move up in management positions, they gain the confidence to make decisions to drive business. Therefore, women who move to C-suite positions have the confidence to make adventurous business decisions.

Given the opportunity women include preparation to advance to the C-suite. Zenger and Folkman (2012) found no substantial evidence that women are incapable of operating at the profit / loss end of business. Rather, women given hard business roles demonstrate great competency and skill. In spite of the Pew findings that gender does not play a role in a person's ability to lead, most Americans say it is easier for men to get into top leadership positions in business as well as politics. The McKinsey, *Women in the Workplace* (2015) study found women are almost three times more likely than men to say they have personally missed an assignment, promotion, or raise because of their gender. Compared with men, women also report that they are consulted less often on important decisions. It is not surprising therefore that two-thirds of Americans overall believe men have an advantage and three-quarters of women indicate men have a better chance for advancement (McKinsey, 2015).

The research proves women are competent visionary relationship builders who embody trust and integrity as components in their leadership. In spite of many deterring factors women leaders exude confidence to achieve self-actualization. Women bring to the leadership table sound characteristics such as flexibility, a sound work ethic, integrity, and good communication skills, all of which are essential factors in effective leadership. In the study *Women Matter,* conducted by McKinsey (2013), the findings determined that gender has an influence on the self-perceptions of leaders. There are as many leadership styles as there are people who see themselves as leaders (Ghaffari, 2001). Additional research cited by Eagly and Carli (2007) indicated that gender norms tend to direct male leaders toward a task-oriented style, and female leaders toward an interpersonally oriented style. The end result of this perception of gender bias continues to create barriers to the advancement of women to senior leadership positions. An argument to be made is that a collaborative holistic approach to leadership would benefit all.

Gender Stereotypes and Bias

There are many reasons for the continual delay of women as leaders in executive positions. A preponderance of research found that women are often excluded from high level managerial positions solely because of perception (McKinsey, 2013; McKinsey & Co., 2015; Zenger & Folkman, 2012). Zenger and Folkman (2012) found the perception is women are care takers and men take charge of the situation. Many traits associated with traditional business culture are considered masculine. These traits include, heroic leadership including individualism, and control, (Isaac, Griffin, & Price, 2010). Women face intense scrutiny far greater than their male counterparts that transcends performance. Often, perceptions include lack of a good cultural fit. Research indicated that societal bias suggests women typically bear a disproportionate amount of responsibility for home and family and cannot provide the required attention in higher level leadership positions. A Pew Research Center report on women and leadership found that 38% of Americans believe one major reason there are not more women in top elective office in the United States is that they are held to higher standards than men. Confirming that discrimination is a factor in the glass ceiling (Hopewell, McNeely, Kuiler, & Hahm, 2009). Leadership is a male domain. Organizational cultural expectations continue to be viewed from a male perspective.

Societal perception transforms into bias in the workplace. McGinn and Tempest, (2010) noted researchers from Columbia's Business School presented information to two groups of students about two entrepreneurs. The information was identical except the gender and names: one female (Heidi) and one male (Howard). The two groups of students were asked personality questions about the two entrepreneurs. Even though both groups of students found that Heidi and Howard were equally competent. Howard was seen as a more likable colleague, while Heidi with the exact same information was seen as selfish and not the type of person one would want to hire or work for (McGinn & Tempest, 2010). This finding exemplifies how men and women continue to perpetuate the biases in the workplace.

There are many venues which continue to perpetuate the inequality of women. The Internet, social media, television, radio, and print all produce *covert,* as well as *overt* messages regarding the portrayal of women. The culture of gender stereotypical mindsets in terms of work and life balance must be examined from a non-judgmental lens. Perhaps society may need to focus attention on fairness, respect and equality, essential components of building harmonious, cooperative, and productive workplaces. One can contribute to a fair and equitable work environment one action at a time. Perhaps one will not categorize a little girl playing with three little boys as bossy, because of taking the leadership role in the group. Perhaps, as a man in the next meeting when Jane makes a suggestion that seems to go unnoticed or not heard, Dick will say I think Jane has made a viable suggestion. Instead of restating Jane's suggestion and taking the credit.

The stereotypical gender roles society dictates for men and women can preclude women from membership in certain clubs and gyms where elite male leaders meet. Research indicated that some women adopt hard and aggressive demeanors, talk sport, and suppress authentic female characteristics in order to be accepted in male dominated leadership circles ("Women in the Workplace," 2015). While women recognize the importance and potential of networking, they are often absent from opportunities such as drinks at the club or on the golf course. Women simply do not have the same social access as their male counterparts (Ely, Ibarra, & Kolb, 2011).

Ryan, Haslam, Hersby, and Bongiorno (2011) suggested that as some women break through the *glass ceiling,* they find themselves on the *glass cliff*. The glass cliff is when women are offered leadership roles under risky and precarious circumstances (Ryan et al., 2011). When accepting these leadership positions, the odds of failure are often higher. In their research, Ryan et al. (2011) found women who are successful in reversing the negative situation oftentimes reassigned to another position and a man is given the position, which is now stable.

Shattering the Glass Ceiling

Ryan et al. (2011) suggested improvement in gender bias and expectations must become transparent to change our stereotypes. Ryan et al. also encouraged networking with established women leaders in one's field and practicing a work-life balance to make the most strategic use of time. Chelette (2013) posited that women must let go of negative embedded stereotypes and treat other women with respect and admiration. Sally Helgesen (2016) suggested women leaders focus on what they have to contribute to an organization, rather than how they need to change and adapt to an organization. Helgesen and Johnson (2010) studied successful women leaders and identified five unique qualities that they have to offer to include the a) quality of relationships; b) bias for direct communication; c) lead from the center not from the top; d) comfortable with diversity; and e) skilled at integrating their personal and professional lives.

Compelling arguments have been made for why one need to rethink leadership development and selection of those at the helm (Chelette, 2013; Ghaffari, 2011; Helgesen & Johnson, 2010; Ryan et al., 2011). Women demonstrated the ability to analyze information in a broader social context. However, this finding may lend itself to not being heard and the perception that there are no strategies to achieve the vision. Helgesen (2016) recommended that to remain authentic and aware of communication styles one must ensure one is heard. She found there was a gap between high-level male leaders who did not think that women had the capacity for vision and strategy and women's perception of their vision and strategies, which were very positive. This finding may be because of the communication style of how information is presented.

Gender differences in communication style may contribute to misunderstandings and tension. Helgesen (2016) advised that women should know their audience when making presentations, and be sure to articulate the facts, framing them in a clear, and concise manner to ensure that the audience is comfortable in receiving the information. In other words, women must present the statistical data first for analytical concrete thinkers. Ending with for example, "I found some interesting relationship correlations that may impact our division. If you are interested I would be glad to share my findings with you when time permits." This communication approach suggests one is aware of the business climate and present in the moment (Ghaffari, 2011). Practicing this style increases the presenters' suggested vision and ensures strategies will be heard.

In summary, leadership skills must be developed and nurtured. There seems to be a lack of mentoring to develop leadership skills among women moving up the corporate ladder. Other barriers and challenges women face in their development as leaders pertains to work-life balance, lack of role models, lack of opportunities for career advancement, and a lack of support from upper management. Women are less supportive of other women. Organizations must begin a cultural shift to embrace diversity, while enhancing, and supporting the career paths of female leaders.

Conclusion

The implications for social change include enhanced awareness among senior management. Forward thinking and a willingness to collaborate and compromise continue to be needed for meaningful change when it comes to challenging stereotypes. Collaborative male and female leadership could result in increased revenue, increased productivity, and heightened organizational efficiency. The undervaluation of women is still deeply embedded in many workplaces; by eliminating bias employers create leadership.

As active change agents we must reflect on how women are portrayed. Women must speak out regarding women's objectification in the media. In the wake of female leadership at the helm of the UN, as well as potentially for the most powerful country in the world, we as a society must continue to seek equality in higher-level leadership. To make a significant social justice contribution to break through the proverbial glass ceiling, one must be reflective thinkers of our actions. We must engage in meaningful conversations around issues of equality, race, ethnicity, ability, status, and sexual orientation.

THOUGHTS FROM THE ACADEMIC ENTREPRENEUR

The problem to be solved:

- Understand the factors contributing to the under-representation of women in executive level management positions.

The goals:

- Analyze and identify salary gaps between men and women in higher-level management positions.
- Understanding *covert,* as well as *overt* barriers women face in obtaining executive level management roles.
- Identify the characteristics and leadership styles of women.
- Illuminate communication styles of female and male leaders.
- Recognize the benefits of female leadership.

The questions to ask:

- Why do women remain underrepresented and face barriers to the top leadership positions?
- What are the competencies that are needed to overcome the gender bias and stereotypes that women encounter in the workplace?
- What interventions can corporations implement to ensure the opportunity for leadership positions for women?
- What steps can corporations utilize to ensure equal salaries between male and female employees?

Today's Business Application:

- Collaborative male and female leadership may result in increased revenue, greater productivity, and heightened organizational efficiency.
- Organizations must begin a cultural shift to embrace diversity, enhance, embrace and support the career paths of female leaders.

REFERENCES

Bhasin, K. (2011). Here's the philosophy PepsiCo CEO Indra Nooyi uses to lead her cohorts. *Business Insider.* Retrieved from http://www.businessinsider.com/pepsico-ceo-indra-nooyi-five-cs-leadership-2011-8

Chamie, J. (2014). Women more educated than men but still paid less. *Yale Global.* Retrieved from http://yaleglobal.yale.edu/content/women-more-educated-men-still-paid-less-men

Chelette, B. (2013). *The women's code presents: Happy women happy world.* Los Angeles, CA: Visualist Publishing.

Cook, A., & Glass, C. (2011). Leadership change and shareholder value: How markets react to the appointments of women. *Human Resource Management, 50,* 501–519. doi:10.1002/hrm.20438

Eagly, A., & Carli, L. (2007). *Through the labyrinth.* Boston, MA: Harvard Business School Press.

Ely, R. J., Ibarra, H., & Kolb, D. M. (2011). Taking gender into account: Theory and design for women's leadership development programs. *Academy of Management Learning & Education, 10,* 474–493. doi:10.5465/amle.2010.0046

Ghaffari, E. (2011). *Women leaders at work.* Berkeley, CA: Apress.

Helgesen, S. (2016) Say it loud. *Strategy & Business.* Retrieved from http://www.strategy-business.com/blog/Say-It-Loud

Helgesen, S., & Johnson, J. (2010). *The female vision: Women's real power at work.* San Francisco, CA: Berrett-Koehler.

Hopewell, L., McNeely, C. L., Kuiler, E. W., & Hahm, J. (2009). University leaders and the public agenda: Talking about women and diversity in STEM fields. *Review of Policy Research, 26,* 589–607. doi:10.1111/j.1541-1338.2009.00407.x

Hunt, V., Layton, D., & Price, S. (2015). *Diversity matters.* New York, NY: McKinsey & Company.

Isaac, C., Griffin, L., & Carnes, M. (2010). A qualitative study of faculty members' views of women chairs. *Journal of Women's Health, 19,* 533–546. doi:10.1089/jwh.2009.1506

Lopez-Zafra, E., Garcia-Retamero, R., & Berrios Martos, M. P. (2012). The relationship between transformational leadership and emotional intelligence from a gendered approach. *Psychological Record, 62*(1), 97–114. Retrieved from https://www.researchgate.net/publication/225026150_The_Relationship_between_Transformational_Leadership_and_Emotional_Intelligence_from_a_Gendered_Approach

McGinn, K. L., & Tempest, N. (2010) Heidi Roizen. *Harvard Business School Case 800–228*. Retrieved from https://hbr.org/product/heidi-roizen/800228-PDF-ENG

McKinsey & Co. (2013). *Women Matter 2013: Gender diversity in top management: Moving corporate culture, moving boundaries*. Retrieved from http://www.mckinsey.com/global-themes/women-matter

McKinsey & Company & LeanIn.Org. (*2015) Women in the workplace 2015*. Retrieved from http://womenintheworkplace.com/

McMillen, S. G. (2008). *Seneca Falls and the origins of the women's rights movement*. New York, NY: Oxford University Press.

Obama, B. (2014) Full transcript: Obama's 2014 State of the Union address. *The Washington Post*. Retrieved from https://www.washingtonpost.com/politics/full-text-of-obamas-2014-state-of-the-union-address/2014/01/28/e0c93358-887f-11e3-a5bd-844629433ba3_story.html

Pew Research Center. (2015). *Women and leadership: Public says women are equally qualified, but barriers persist*. Retrieved from http://www.pewsocialtrends.org/2015/01/14/women-and-leadership/

Rao, M. S. (2014). *Manage your boss with hard skills: Lead your boss with soft skill training*. Retrieved from https://trainingmag.com/manage-your-boss-hard-skills-lead-your-boss-soft-skills

Rosen, C. (2015). Patricia Arquette clarifies Oscar night comments. *The Huffington Post*. Retrieved from http://www.huffingtonpost.com/2015/03/04/patricia-arquette-oscar-comments_n_6798978.html

Ryan, M. K.; Haslam, S. A.; Hersby, M. D.; & Bongiorno, R. (2011). Think crisis–think female: The glass cliff and contextual variation in the think manager–think male stereotype. *Journal of Applied Psychology, 96*, 470–484. doi:10.1037/a0022133

Schuh, S. S., Hernandez Bark, A., Van Quaquebeke, N., Hossiep, R., Frieg, P., & Dick, R. (2014). Gender differences in leadership role occupancy: The mediating role of power motivation. *Journal of Business Ethics, 120*, 363–379. doi:10.1007/s10551-013-1663-9

Thompson, R. (2015). Women and leadership around the world. In S. R. Madsen, F. Ngunjiri, Wambura, K. A. Longman, & C. Cherrey, Cynthia (Eds.), *Women and leadership around the world* (pp. 3–22). Retrieved from http://www.infoagepub.com/products/Women-and-Leadership-around-the-World

United Nations (UN). (2003). *Millennium development goals*. Retrieved from http://www.un.org/millenniumgoals/

United Nations (UN). (2005). *Division for the advancement of women.* Retrieved from http://www.un.org/womenwatch/daw/daw/

United Nations (UN). (2016). *Women facts and figures: Leadership and political participation.* Retrieved from:http://www.unwomen.org/en/what-we-do/leadership-and-political-participation/facts-and-figures

U.S. Bureau of Labor Statistics (BLS). (2015). *BLS reports women in the labor force: A databook.* Retrieved from http://www.bls.gov/opub/reports/womens-databook/archive/women-in-the-labor-force-a-databook-2015.pdf

Walker, R. C., & Aritz, J. (2015). Women doing leadership: Leadership styles and organizational culture. *International Journal of Business Communication, 52,* 452–478. doi:10.1177/2329488415598429

Zenger, J., & Folkman, J. (2012). Are women better leaders than men? *Harvard Business* Review. Retrieved from https://hbr.org/2012/03/a-study-in-leadership-women-do

About the Author...

Dr. Denise Mayo Moore Resides in Southwestern Tennessee. Dr. Denise holds several accredited degrees; a Bachelor of Professional Studies in Human Studies from Metropolitan College of New York, Master of Science: Community Economic Development from Southern New Hampshire University, Masters in Social Work (MSW) from Yeshiva University, Ph.D. in Psychology from Walden University.

Dr. Denise holds the distinction of being appointed the first women Director of the Bachelor in Social Work program at Touro University Worldwide, where she is a full Faculty Member. Dr. Denise passionately nurtures students to become reflective practitioners of change. Dr. Denise designed and implemented the curriculum for the Bachelor of Social Work Program. She serves on the Academic Council, Accreditation Committee and Chairwomen of the University Curriculum Committee.

MOORE FOR YOUR NEEDS was created in 1995 to provide support for nonprofit organizations in the areas of board development, fund-raising, and SWOT analysis. MOORE FOR YOUR NEEDS provides consulting to students of all ages to make the right decisions regarding education. We keep students focused and on task throughout their educational experience.

To reach Dr. Denise Mayo Moore for information on consulting or coaching services please e-mail: denise@mooreforyourneeds.org

8

Innovative Strategies for Women to Overcome Barriers in Pursuing Leadership Roles in Healthcare Organizations

Dr. Jennifer Guerguis & Dr. Kirlos M. Guerguis

Background on Healthcare Organizational Change

The background on healthcare organizational change, is summed up in one word, *chaotic*. The Patient Protection and Affordable Care Act (PPACA) is drastically changing the healthcare industry. President Barack Obama with the signing of the PPACA also known as Obamacare mandated healthcare exchanges across the nation. Additional PPACA changes include the modification to patient care, payment structures, healthcare infrastructure, and the requirement for individuals to possess healthcare insurance (Guerguis, 2014). The future holds more changes for healthcare organizations, organizations that successfully navigate have the best chance to succeed. The purpose of this article is to address the lack of women in leadership roles in healthcare organizations managing organizational change. Healthcare organizations need to start finding innovative ways that use refractive thinking strategies to address the lack of women in leadership roles.

The healthcare industry remains forever changing because of the PPACA, the changes are broad and chaotic (Guerguis, 2014). The forever changing environment is the new norm. Countless innovations exist which are driven from the U.S. government, healthcare insurance systems, hospital systems, healthcare providers, nonprofits, and consumers. Healthcare organizations during this changing landscape must maintain their levels of care while at the same time be participants and drivers of innovation (Johnson, Sanders, & Stange, 2014). Women in healthcare leadership possess the skills and traits necessary for the changing healthcare industry.

Healthcare leaders must also balance many competing components striving for their attention. These competing components include delivering cost effective care, dealing with provider motivations, and ensuing clients receive adequate care in a timely manner. The PPACA is expanding these components to include the investigation into new models of care, new models of reimbursement, new approaches to patient satisfaction, and new models of healthcare infrastructure (Guerguis, 2014). All this change is both difficult to track and understand, yet as leaders, we are all required to continue to grow and improve our organizations.

Background of Challenges to Organizational Change

To understand the challenges of organizational change, one must first understand the different types of organizational change. Two types of organizational change exist, *administrative* and *technical* (Austin & Claassen, 2008). Administrative organizational change is the process and technical organizational change is the product as a result of the process. The topic of healthcare organizational change encompasses both types of change, which makes the process more complex.

One challenge is readiness to organizational change. The chaotic changing healthcare landscape severely limits the readiness capabilities of healthcare organizations. Healthcare organizations are thrust into the fray and must quickly address the issues of healthcare organizational change without the needed time to study and prepare for the change. Healthcare leaders need to work towards closing the gap between a lack of readiness and the need to plan for organizational change (Saxton & Finkelstein, 2012).

Another challenge is resistance to organizational change, which is a larger issue when the organization is ill prepared (Guerguis, 2015). A higher level of resistance exists to healthcare organizational change since the PPACA is politically driven as opposed to being driven by the healthcare industry. The complexities of the various providers with differing positions, levels of education, years of experience, areas of expertise, and differing perceptions of healthcare in general adds to the challenges leaders face when implementing change (Guerguis, 2015). Leaders need to find innovative ways to address this resistance.

How Is Healthcare Organizational Change Different?

What distinguishes healthcare organizational change from other types of organizational change? The simple answer is that the consequences are much higher when people's lives are at stake. As a result, leaders tend to take much longer in making decisions because of the numerous levels of complexity. The first level of complexity is the choices healthcare providers make leads to dire consequence that involve people's health. Each person is unique and has unique healthcare wants and needs, but healthcare systems in 2016 use a standardized system approach lacking distinctiveness. Any changes to that system may have dire consequences toward each person unique situation. The PPACA mandates that organizations address each person's unique healthcare outcomes, but the current healthcare system service delivery approach must change to include an increase in flexibility (Guerguis, 2014). In the mental health setting these complexities further exacerbate because less flexibility exists with the types of service delivery and the knowledge of mental health illness is less understood than physical illnesses (Corrigan, Morris, Michaels, Rafacz, & Rüsch, 2012). Women leaders can help manage healthcare change in a distinctive manner.

The healthcare industry has a dismal record of accomplishment using resources to implement organizational change. Approximately, 240 billion is spent on healthcare research and 85% of this funding is misspent by healthcare organizations (Chalmers et al., 2014). The bulk of healthcare funding is spent on discovering new cures for illnesses and little to fund meaningful organizational changes. The chaotic nature of healthcare is a consequence because of the lack of funding, which focuses on meaningful organizational change that affects both the patient and the provider. A paradigm shift must occur in the mind of policy makers and funders, policy makers need to create more opportunities for growth and change in the other parts of the healthcare system not solely on the patient.

Background of Women as Healthcare Leaders

A serious problem exists regarding women achieving leadership roles in the healthcare industry. Although women hold 74% of the positions in the overall healthcare workforce, a small percentage are at a senior level position (Dunn, 2014). Only 24% of women hold an executive or higher position and even fewer women, only 18%, hold the title of Chief Executive Officer (CEO) (Hauser, 2014). In the ever-changing healthcare industry, the glass ceiling exists for women as healthcare leaders (Nanton, 2015). The glass ceiling for women leaders worsens by women leaders who refuse to provide guidance and support to other women because of a fear of perceived favoritism.

Women need to work through various challenges, one challenge is the lack of women role models in senior executive positions. If women cannot see themselves as leaders, there is no driving force to get them to strive for these executive positions. Differences exist between the career paths that men and women take in the healthcare industry and this plays a role in having more men holding executive positions. The perception that men have more leadership oriented career paths creates a workplace bias, where society perceives women to not have leadership skills, consequently few earn the opportunity to be leaders.

Workplace biases towards women exist and this leads to women themselves believing these biases and not striving for higher executive positions (Koch, D'Mello, & Sackett, 2015). This self-imposed bias is difficult at times to conquer. If women do not possess the opportunity and receive coaching correctly, women will not transform themselves into leaders. This bias is more prevalent in the mental healthcare industry where women have the perception of being providers and not as leaders.

Advantages Women Bring to Leadership

Women possess unique skills and traits that they make us of when engaging in leadership roles. Women's traits such as compassion, approachability, transparency, and being inclusive are traits a leader must possess. Patience is also another trait that women possess, which allows them to approach difficult situations in a more logical and efficient manner. Women also possess management skills that include a more collaborative style and higher level of empathy, which helps in motivating employees. Women are better skilled than most men at building rapport, which then leads to employees feeling that they are part of the decision making process (Fontenot, 2012). Another skill that women possess that adds to workplace comradery is women openly vet and share their ideas with other employees. Women also have the mental strength to engage and conquer the ingrained biases that exist toward them in the workplace. These combined skills and traits empower women to break the glass ceiling to leadership and bridge the gap (Fontenot, 2012). In the healthcare industry women typically begin their careers as healthcare providers. This career path provides a unique advantage that allows women to both connect with their coworkers and understand the needs of their patients. This dichotomy allows women to understand the entire healthcare structure as a whole and approach leadership with an advantage.

One trait that further bridges the gap toward women becoming leaders is women's mastery of emotional intelligence. Women who possess emotional intelligence tend to have an increase in their resilience (Jayalakshmi & Magdalin, 2015). Women's advantage is that they understand emotional intelligence in two parts. The first part being the ability to understand and connect with the emotions of others (Hayee & Hassan, 2011). The second part being the ability to self-regulate their own internal emotions (Hayee & Hassan, 2011). The first emotional intelligence ability helps women to connect emotionally with others, which dramatically increases their approachability. Employees would prefer going to a leader that is going to better empathize with their emotions and / or unique circumstances. The second emotional intelligence ability allows women to be calm and collected regardless of the types of stressful and chaotic situations that may arise in the workplace. This ability helps women leaders keep their employees focused during stressful situations. In the healthcare industry where stressful situations can lead to the loss of patients' lives, women's emotional intelligence helps them lead others to saving lives. Women can better read nonverbal cues, which helps them be problem solvers (Gulabovska & Leeson, 2014). They can be proactive and reactive at problem solving.

Women's ability to understand verbal, visual, and emotional factors relates to them being better communicators. Women are naturally neurologically different from men, women are more inclined to use both the left and right hemispheres of their brains (Ahmadi, Ahmadlou, Rezazade, Azad-Marzabadi, & Sajedi, 2013). Because of the neurological difference, women achieve higher scores in oral and written evaluations than men. Enhanced communication abilities of women make them relationship specialists. Communication is a tool women use to create genuine and meaningful relationships in the workplace. Women also use communication as a tool to network with others, which allows for the location of opportunities that they overlook. Women are also better communication experts because they are clear on the outcomes they want to achieve. In the healthcare industry where communication can be the difference between whether a patience lives or dies, women leaders better handle the most stressing of situations.

How Women Bridge the Gap to Leadership

Self-belief that all women possess the skillset to become a leader in any workplace environment is a way for women to bridge the leadership gap. The lack of women's self-belief leads to a perceived confidence gap. This lack of women's self-belief equates to a lower level of self-esteem. In an eight-year study conducted in 2015, over 985,000 men and women across 48 nations were questioned about the issue of self-esteem, women scored lower than men as in relation to their self-esteem (Bleidorn et al., 2015). Women's issues with self-esteem is a universal problem that needs attention. One method to bridge this gap could be for women to reach out to other women who hold a senior executive positon for mentoring purposes. The goal of the mentoring process would be to impart learned and experienced knowledge as well as increased the level of self-esteem. The goal would be that under proper guidance, women can reach senior executive positions.

Societal norms dramatically changed from the perception that a woman's place is only in the home and not a source of income, to the main source of income for a majority of households. The social norm still present in 2016 is that women have no place in leadership roles (Nanton, 2015). One way women break this social norm is to not be afraid to challenge themselves to strive for leadership roles. A study by Goswami and Gupta (2012) found that women's perception of sex discrimination lead to lower job satisfaction and low self-esteem. When society tells women that they cannot be leaders, they can use this discriminatory behavior as a driving force to contest and to not conform to these discriminatory social norms. Regardless of the number of time women are discriminated against, they must perceiver and continually push for change and not relent. Women should use all available workplace resources, such as their workplace union or professional organizations to fight back when being discriminated against because of gender. Regardless of how gender or workplace discrimination occurs, discrimination is wrong and women should not tolerate such behaviors irrespective from whom it originates (Schmitt, Branscombe, Postmes, & Garcia, 2014).

Another way women bridge this gap to leadership starts early on where women choose their career paths. In 2016, we have the first female candidate for U.S. president and there are countless other female world leaders. These groundbreaking women understood early on that they were leaders or had the capacity to lead. From an early age, woman must possess the confidence to strive to be the corner office executive or the renowned leader. The misnomer that women must attend the most prestigious institutions of learning still exists. Regardless of the learning institute that women attend, steady focus on a career path with goals oriented toward leadership ultimately wins. An advantageous career path to reaching a leadership position is selecting and finding a good organization where women work their way up the ladder. This process of locating an organization is easier as time elapses, but is still a challenge to find organizations whose structure is culturally sensitive to view and accept women as leaders.

Women need to take more risks in the decision-making process. At a young age, society teaches women that risky behavior is dangerous and that perfection is what should be strived. This risk aversion behavior leads women to be uncomfortable and avoid situations that require risk taking (Dalborg, von Friedrichs & Wincent, 2015). Under high stress situations, neurologically, women take less risk than men (Mather & Lighthall, 2012). This neurological inclination can be a setback for women as they pursue leadership positions. Women do not need to blindly take risks but they also should not be complacent. Women need to take calculated risks as leaders. Women struggle with more challenges they need to overcome and are fearful of making mistakes that could reflect poorly on them as leaders (Humbert & Brindley, 2015). So as a result, women are less likely to take risks as leaders. Women that hold leadership positions have learned through their mistakes and this is the message that women pursuing leadership roles need to learn. IT IS OK TO MAKE MISTAKES. Unless the mistake directly relates to a person's life, women need to take more risks and experience mistakes so they can learn and grow from those mistakes.

Women Leader's Advantages in Healthcare Changes

The healthcare environment experiences drastic levels of change not since Medicare and Medicaid passed in 1965 (Guerguis, 2014). With all these widespread changes in the healthcare industry, all types of healthcare organizations need women to hold a more prominent role. As discussed earlier, women possess a wide range of skills and traits that they utilize to help healthcare organizations survive and adapt to the changing landscape (Marques, 2011). The management and deployment of effective organizational change is the cornerstone for healthcare organizations to navigate the changing landscape, women should be part of the leadership team taking on this challenge.

The PPACA and internal healthcare drivers for efficiency are leading to organizations and employees resisting change (Guerguis, 2014). Resistance to organizational change is a huge challenge that leaders need to address (Guerguis, 2015). An innovative method to address the challenge to resistance to organizational change is to have women spearheading the process. Women hold crucial traits such as communication skills that aid in building rapport with employees and are better collaborators (Marques, 2011). Women are able to build trust with employees and make the employees collaborators to the changes taking place. Women vet and share in the decision making process, which decreases employee's anxiety and resistance to organizational change. Organizational strategic change increases with the involvement of women leaders (Triana, Miller, & Trzebiatowski, 2013). Healthcare organization need women who portray that they are partners with others in solving the problems faced by healthcare organization because of the need to change.

The social architecture within organizations needs strategical change by current leaders for organizations to start seeing women as leaders (Nanton, 2015). Healthcare organizations that hold greater gender equity practices as part of their culture will be more likely to have women in high-level positions. For healthcare organizations culture to change, they need to start eliminating current workplace biases. Women who value diversity receive lower performance ratings in the workplace which increases workplace biases. (Hekman, Johnson, Der Foo, & Yang, 2016). Healthcare leaders need to start identifying women within their organization who hold such leadership traits and create career paths that will allow attainment of leadership roles. This identification process should start with women at all levels of the organization, because leaders need to evaluate all women for the uniqueness they bring to the culture.

An effective leader of organizational change must understand both the logical and emotional factors associated with employees as healthcare companies undergo organizational change. Women leaders are predisposed to having an advantage over men because of their emotional intelligence. Emotional intelligence is a skill that is innate to women. A leader who has mastered emotional intelligence possess transformational leadership skills (Lopez-Zafra, Garcia-Retamero, & Martos, 2012). The chaotic healthcare landscape is in vital need of transformational leaders and women can attain these roles. Women as transformational leaders in a healthcare environment are able to understand the logical and emotional needs of employees and patients (Lopez-Zafra et al., 2012). As the saying goes, sometimes the situation needs a woman's touch. Healthcare organizations increase their likelihood of successfully using transformational leaders by acknowledging and identifying women in their organization.

A nurturing and inclusive workplace environment in healthcare organizations can decrease the hurdles in achieving meaningful change. A woman leader's ability to use the feminine trait of nurturing in a workplace environment is a unique skill (Bullough & de Luque, 2015). Women's nurturing skill is not a weakness, but a strength that conveys as being fair and just, while holding people accountable. Women's nurturing and supportive traits motivate employees in organizations (Harvey, 2015). Women leaders who possess a nurturing nature are able to connect with others and lead with a collaborative leadership style. Healthcare organizations that have nurturing women leaders empower other employees to find solutions for complex problems with minimal risk for retaliation if errors occur. Women leaders nurturing skills allows them to create in-depth and complex relationships regardless of the employee's position in a healthcare organization. Women leaders using their nurturing traits are also adept at creating teams that can tackle complex and multidimensional healthcare problems (Bullough & de Luque, 2015).

Conclusion

Healthcare organizational change is chaotic because of laws such as the PPACA. The challenges of organizational change are readiness to change and resistance to change. Healthcare organizational change differs from typical organizational change because healthcare organizations are unique and complex when their decisions can affect people's lives. Women are essential to the successful execution of overall healthcare change.

Women face a wide variety of challenges; one is the lack of women leaders. This lack of women leaders impedes other women from reaching senior executive roles. More women are working in healthcare, but more men hold senior level positions. Women encounter various social and workplace biases that continue to evolve, lack of women leaders shows a gap that needs bridging (Ramakiran, 2014). Gender discrimination although decreasing still exists. Women have to persevere challenge biases to advance in their careers.

Women hold valuable qualities and traits that make them excellent leaders. Some of the traits that women possess over men include, empathy, openness, transparency, inclusiveness, nurturing, and adept communication skills (Marques, 2011). Possessing such traits is not enough and women must attain the drive and self-belief that they can attain leadership roles regardless of the healthcare organizations that employ them. Women are also encouraged to take risks, learn, and grow from any mistakes.

Healthcare organizations would greatly benefit from having more women leaders that possess crucial leadership traits. The social architecture needs to change in order for women to attain opportunities for leadership roles. Healthcare organizations need transformational leaders and women meet this need because they possess emotional intelligence. Women's nurturing ability aids to create a workplace environment that is fair and just.

Bridging the women's healthcare leadership gap is a twofold problem. The first problem is that women must have the internal fortitude to strive to be leaders. The second problem is that healthcare organizations must eliminate any obstacle to women transforming into leaders. A unique recommendation to aspiring women leaders is to connect with female leaders around the world in the digital age using tools such as www.thumbtack.com and / or www.noomii.com. Aspiring women leaders can use these refractive thinking tools for career and life coaching, which ultimately helps gain the internal fortitude to become the next leading woman in healthcare.

THOUGHTS FROM THE ACADEMIC ENTREPRENEUR

The problem to be solved:

- Severe shortage of women leaders in healthcare.
- Women not perceiving themselves as leaders and organizations not availing leadership opportunities to women.

The goals:

- Understanding women's leadership traits to implement organizational healthcare industry change broadly and effectively.

The questions to ask:

- Are there any healthcare centric leadership traits that women possess?
- What advantages do women leaders have to manage and lead healthcare change?
- Do any challenges/obstacles exist specifically for women leaders in organizational healthcare change?

Today's Business Application:

- How healthcare organizations can enable women to be leaders.
- Women effectively understanding and harnessing their traits in the midst of healthcare organizational change.

REFERENCES

Ahmadi, K., Ahmadlou, M., Rezazade, M., Azad-Marzabadi, E., & Sajedi, F. (2013). Brain activity of women is more fractal than men. *Neuroscience Letters, 535*, 7–11. doi:10.1016/j.neulet.2012.12.043

Austin, M. J., & Claassen, J. (2008). Impact of organizational change on organizational culture: Implications for introducing evidence-based practice. *Journal of Evidence-Based Social Work, 5*, 321–359. doi:10.1300/J394v05n01_12

Bleidorn, W., Arslan, R. C., Denissen, J. J. A., Rentfrow, P. J., Gebauer, J. E., Potter, J., & Gosling, S. D. (2015). Age and gender differences in self-esteem: A cross-cultural window. *Journal of Personality and Social Psychology, 109*(6). doi:10.1037/pspp000007

Bullough, A., & de Luque, M. S. (2015). Women's participation in entrepreneurial and political leadership: The importance of culturally endorsed implicit leadership theories. *Leadership, 11*(1), 36–56. doi:10.1177/1742715013504427:

Chalmers, I., Bracken, M. B., Djulbegovic, B., Garattini, S., Grant, J., & Gülmezoglu, A. M. (2014). How to increase value and reduce waste when research priorities are set. *Lancet, 383*(9912), 156–165. doi:10.1016/S0140-6736(13)62229-1.

Corrigan, P. W., Morris, S. B., Michaels, P. J., Rafacz, J. D., & Rüsch, N. (2012). Challenging the public stigma of mental illness: A meta-analysis of outcome studies. *Psychiatric Services, 63*, 963–973. doi:10.1176/appi.ps.201100529

Dalborg, C., von Friedrichs, Y., & Wincent, J. (2015). Risk perception matters: why women's passion may not lead to a business start-up. *International Journal of Gender and Entrepreneurship, 7*(1), 87–104. doi:10.1108/IJGE-01-2013-0001

Dunn, L. (2014, April 24). Women's executive leadership still lags, and it matters more in healthcare than other industries. *The Daily Beat Blog.* Retrieved from http://www.beckershospitalreview.com/healthcare-blog/women-s-executive-leadership-still-lags-and-it-matter-more-in-healthcare-than-other-industries.html

Fontenot, T. (2012). Leading ladies: women in healthcare leadership. *Frontiers of Health Services Management, 28*(4), 11–21. Retrieved from http://www.ache.org/pubs/Frontiers/frontiers_index.cfm

Goswami, S., & Gupta, H. N. (2012). Perception of sex discrimination at workplace and psychological consequences of women at work. *Social Science International, 28*(1), 93–104. Retrieved from http://www.mdppl.in/node/2379

Guerguis, J. (2015). *Mental health therapists' attitudes on adoption of evidence-based practices and organizational culture* (Doctoral dissertation). Retrieved from ProQuest Dissertations and Theses Database. (UMI No. 3702074)

Guerguis, K. M. (2014). *The Affordable Care Act implications for community mental health organizations* (Doctoral dissertation). Retrieved from ProQuest Dissertations and Theses Database. (UMI No. 3646630)

Guerrero, E. G., Padwa, H., Fenwick, K., Harris, L. M., & Aarons, G. A. (2016). Identifying and ranking implicit leadership strategies to promote evidence-based practice implementation in addiction health services. *Implementation Science, 11*(69), 1–13. doi:10.1186/s13012-016-0438-y

Gulabovska, M., & Leeson, P. (2014). Why are women better decoders of nonverbal language? *Gender Issues, 31*(3–4), 202–218. doi:10.1007/s12147-014-9127-9

Harvey, S. (2015). Transcultural women leaders. *SAM Advanced Management Journal, 80*(1), 12–19. Retrieved from http://samnational.org/publications/sam-advanced-management-journal/

Hauser, M. C. (2014). Leveraging women's leadership talent in healthcare. *Journal of Healthcare Management, 59*, 318–322. Retrieved from https://www.ache.org/pubs/jhm/jhm_index.cfm

Hayee, A. A., & Hassan, B. (2011). Self-regulation as predictor of decision making styles among managers of cellular companies. *Pakistan Journal of Psychological Research, 26*(1), 43–60. Retrieved from http://www.pjprnip.edu.pk/pjpr/index.php/pjpr

Hekman, D. R., Johnson, S., Der Foo, M., & Yang, W. (2016). Does diversity-valuing behavior result in diminished performance ratings for nonwhite and female leaders? *Academy of Management Journal, 59*(2), 1–59. Retrieved from http://aom.org/amj/

Humbert, A. L., & Brindley, C. (2015). Challenging the concept of risk in relation to women's entrepreneurship. *Gender in Management: An International Journal, 30*(1), 2–25. doi:10.1108/GM-10-2013-0120

Jayalakshmi, V., & Magdalin, S. (2015). Emotional intelligence, resilience and mental health of women college students. *Journal of Psychosocial Research, 10*, 401–408. Retrieved from http://www.mdppl.in/journal/journal-psychosocial-research

Johnson, T. J., Sanders, D. H., & Stange, J. L. (2014). The affordable care act for behavioral health consumers and families. *Journal of Social Work in Disability & Rehabilitation, 13*(1–2), 110–121. doi:10.1080/1536710X.2013.870517

Koch, A. J., D'Mello, S. D., & Sackett, P. R. (2015). A meta-analysis of gender stereotypes and bias in experimental simulations of employment decision making. *Journal of Applied Psychology, 100*(1), 128. doi:10.1037/a0036734

Lopez-Zafra, E., Garcia-Retamero, R., & Martos, M. P. B. (2012). The relationship between transformational leadership and emotional intelligence from a gendered approach. *The Psychological Record, 62*(1), 97. Retrieved from http://thepsychologicalrecord.siu.edu/

Marques, J. (2011). The female awakened leader: Connecting with the inner-sage. *Interbeing, 5*(2), 23–29. Retrieved from http://www.interbeing.biz/

Mather, M., & Lighthall, N. R. (2012). Both risk and reward are processed differently in decisions made under stress. *Current Directions in Psychological Science, 21*(2), 36–41. doi:10.1177/0963721411429452

Nanton, C. R. (2015). Shaping leadership culture to sustain future generations of women leaders. *Journal of Leadership, Accountability, and Ethics, 12*(3), 92–112. Retrieved from http://www.na-businesspress.com/jlaeopen.html

Ramakiran. (2014). The challenge of equality at work. *Indian Journal of Commerce and Management Studies, 5*(3), 117–121. Retrieved from http://www.scholarshub.net/ijcms.html

Saxton, J. W., & Finkelstein, M. M. (2012). Be prepared in the post-PPACA liability and healthcare environment: assure, do not assume. *The Journal of Medical Practice Management, 28*(2), 101–105. Retrieved from http://www.mpmnetwork.com/section_47_MPM-Journal.cfm

Schmitt, M. T., Branscombe, N. R., Postmes, T., & Garcia, A. (2014). The consequences of perceived discrimination for psychological well-being: a meta-analytic review. *Psychological Bulletin, 140*, 921. Retrieved from http://www.apa.org/pubs/journals/bul/

Triana, M. D. C., Miller, T. L., & Trzebiatowski, T. M. (2013). The double-edged nature of board gender diversity: Diversity, firm performance, and the power of women directors as predictors of strategic change. *Organization Science, 25*, 609–632. doi:10.1287/orsc.2013.0842

About the Authors...

Dr. Jennifer Guerguis resides in Eastvale, California. Dr. Jennifer holds several accredited degrees; a Bachelor of Arts (BA) in Psychology from the University of California, Irvine; a Master of Arts (MA) in Psychology with an emphasis in Marriage and Family Therapy from Chapman University; and a Doctorate of Philosophy (PhD) in Organizational Psychology from Walden University.

Dr. Jennifer works as a Licensed Marriage and Family Therapist at Kaiser Permanente. Dr. Jennifer provides therapeutic services to a wide array of individuals. Aside from providing direct patient care, Dr. Jennifer is an active member of a review committee, which provides quality assurance. Dr. Jennifer has enjoyed providing patient care to various populations for the last ten years. She is a member of the International Honor Society in Psychology.

Dr. Jennifer's doctoral study, *Mental Health Therapists' Attitudes on Adoption of Evidence-Based Practices and Organizational Culture*, provided her the opportunity to gain professional and academic expertise to facilitate improvements in mental health organizations.

To reach Dr. Jennifer Guerguis for consulting or guest speaking, please e-mail: jennifer@jguerguis.com

Dr. Kirlos M. Guerguis holds several accredited degrees; a Bachelor of Science in Computer Information Systems (BS) from the DeVry University; a Master of Business Administration in Technology Management (MBA) from Walden University; and a Doctorate of Business Administration (DBA) in Healthcare Administration from Walden University.

Dr. Kirlos, is a seasoned healthcare executive who has held numerous senior executive roles in multiple healthcare organizations. Dr. Kirlos also runs a successful healthcare consulting firm that specializes in finding solutions to complex healthcare problems. Dr. Kirlos is also the co-founder and owner of Quandary Collaborative Analytics Inc., a highly specialized company that provides unique and intuitive analytical dashboards to healthcare organizations.

Dr. Kirlos' doctoral study, *The Affordable Care Act Implications for Community Mental Health Organizations,* provided him the opportunity to gain professional and academic expertise to facilitate improvements in the healthcare and nonprofit industry.

Dr. Kirlos is also an active member of Golden Key International Honour Society.

To reach Dr. Kirlos M. Guerguis for information on consulting, speaking engagements, or any healthcare or healthcare technology topics, please e-mail: kirlos@kguerguis.com

9
A Story of Voice

Dr. Laurie Maslak

The projection of voice as a *human instrument* is a scientific and artistic marvel (Linklater, 1976). Our ability to communicate with each other is a complex physiological interplay of the brain signaling the body to move air in and out through the lungs, diaphragm, vocal cords and nasal passages, resulting in a vibration or resonance. This resonance, when combined with tongue and lip action forms words, phrases, or sounds (in multiple languages) and is truly remarkable. To have others experience these various sounds and words, recognize them, hear, interpret, understand and respond to them is what connects us as human beings (Wheatley, 2005). Whitney and Trosten-Bloom (2003) noted that "human communication and language lie at the center of human organizing and change" (p. 53). Words, language, and metaphors are far more than mere descriptions of reality; they create descriptions of worlds which we experience all around us. Words matter; they literally bring things to life, through what we experience. But how well do we understand the power of voice within the concept of leadership? How does the awareness of an authentic voice contribute to the overall success of a great woman leader? How aware are women leaders of their personal voice and what it really conveys about them as a person, what they stand for, what their vision truly is? Is this awareness different for men or women leaders? Does it need to be?

When one goes to the theater the key attraction is not often the set design, nor the music. It is more often that people are drawn to the theater to hear the actors convey the voice and body movements of a character, who entertains us through a story. The set design and the music are added bonuses to provide context around the message of the story. In many ways, the act of leading others is similar. Followers get behind leaders who can communicate a powerful and engaging message; one in which people are compelled to follow (Clarke & Crossland, 2002). Linklater (1992) challenged all leaders, including female leaders, to consider themselves as actors on a stage and learn to speak a *language of poetry* versus language as a tool. To speak the *language of poetry* is to speak a language of *being* versus *doing;* one that "expresses inner states and emotional responses to outer events. To speak poetry, words must be plugged into the inner condition, generating energy on a vertical path running between mind and heart. They must then be allowed to flow out, fully charged, to the hearer" (Linklater, 1992, p. 30). In this way, words are subjected to every sense (i.e. taste, smell, sight, hearing, and touch), designed to "penetrate and break up patterns of thought. They reach into emotions, memories, associations, and they spark the imagination . . . A consciousness of *how* words are spoken is necessary in cultivating the ability to speak poetically" (Linklater, 1992, p. 31).

As far back as the Italian 14th century, women, such as Christine de Pizan (1404, as cited in Walters, 2005), wrote from the masculine. Later in the 16th century, Shakespeare wrote from perspective of the feminine. The best Shakespearean actors grapple with the ability to convey this feminine voice. As Linklater (1992) stated:

> When words are mainly experienced in the head and the mouth, they convey cerebral meaning. In order to transfer Shakespeare's full emotional, intellectual and philosophical intent from the page to the stage, words much connect with the full human range of intellect and emotion, body and voice. They must be

allowed to rediscover old neuro-physiological routes of appetite to bring back taste and texture to speaking, and to spark the animal response mechanisms which fire creative processes long buried under layers of "civilized' and "rational" behavior. Only the fullest access to the humanity of the speaker allows one to speak Shakespeare fully. (p. 11)

Dr. Carol Gilligan uncovered in her research with developing young women, *In a Different Voice: Psychological Theory and Women's Development* (1982), that women's voices were becoming largely internalized; speaking out for one's self was considered selfish and not culturally accepted. Claiming one's place in a relationship to the rest of society was not condoned, especially if adversarial or controversial in any way. Gilligan's research was heavily influenced by the feminist movement of the late 1960s to late 1970s, in which women fought the historically patriarchal system to have their voices heard. Gilligan argued that it was no longer a question of masculinity versus femininity; instead the focus should be on the quest for understanding the realities and the truths that prevail. Instead, Gilligan noted, it should be a question of voice AND relationship, one supposedly descriptive of the whole human experience. In practice, however, she found that men rarely honored the experience of women, nor spoke for them. She described as "men leaving out women, and women leaving out themselves . . . Creating a "psychic split or inner division of self" (Gilligan, 1982, p. xiii). The different voice, Gilligan described to Wylie (2004), is no longer identified by gender, but by theme. By including women in the voice of the conversation, both women and men hear themselves and one another differently.

In all leadership positions, and as a member of any senior leadership team, the power of each leader's voice is vital. To be left out of the conversation, or more importantly, the decision-making, is to be silenced (Charlesworth, 2005; Ives, 2005). Knowing one's power, and preferred voice type, provides a strategic advantage for any leader (male or female) in securing their place as a valued member of that management team (Charlesworth, 2005). To experience true conversation *that matters,* all unique voices need to be included (Wheatley, 2002).

So how can female leaders discover their authentic personal voice? How does a woman, in a leadership position, project a sense of personal power in her actions and behaviors that reinforce this authentic personal voice? How can the feminine voice provide value within a masculine dominated business environment? These questions resulted in a doctoral study in 2008, which examined the *whole voice* of 12 Senior Human Resource leaders, as members of a specific Senior Management Team (SMT), and their ability to convey the strength, power, confidence and conviction of their leadership, as a valued member of the SMT (Maslak, 2008). The research question asked: *What is the essence of the personal voice, used by a senior Human Resource leader, as a strategic business partner, on the Senior Management Team (SMT)? Is this personal voice authentic to the person or to the culture of the SMT?*

Building on prior studies around *voice* from various dimensions (Aldoory, 1998; Belenky, Clinchy, Goldberger, & Tarule, 1996; Detert & Burris, 2007; Gilligan, 1982, 1993; Helgesen, 1990; Linklater, 1976), this study focused on the connection between the power of voice and leadership presence, when applied to *upper echelon theory* (Hambrick, 2007; Hambrick & Mason, 1984). This particular study included examination of the phenomenon of authentic voice, from the perspectives of language used (*Content*), the way the content is delivered (*Process*), and the presence (*Impact*) on others of the SMT. Searching for the presence of both feminine and masculine voices (Eagly & Carli, 2007; Gilligan, 1993; Helgesen, 1990), within a continued patriarchal business community, and any links between voice and personality preferences, as well as SMT cultural influencers included examination in this doctoral study.

A key result of this study was the formation of individual I poems for each of the 12 senior leaders that were validated with each participant, as a direct representation of the voice they brought to their stories of experiences, on their respective SMTs. The resulting I poem offered individuals the opportunity to hear themselves back through the *language of poetry*. I have since used this reflective method in my coaching of leaders at all levels of the organization and continue to find it useful in helping raise the individual's level of awareness around the content, process of delivery and impact of their messages on others. This remainder of this chapter highlights the value of this technique for women leaders in developing their capacities as change agents and powerful leaders.

I poems

Gilligan (1982) used the I poem in her research on developing women, to "attend to silenced voices and in particular, to pay attention to the multiplicity of a single voice" (as cited in Koelsch, 2016, p. 170). Originally referred to as the *Listening Guide,* this narrative analysis offered the listener with a mechanism for capturing the person's oral experience of their self, while in relationship with a specific event, or activity. The Listening Guide offered a series of specific instructions for analysis of these narratives, obtained through interviews or focus groups (Gilligan, Spencer, Weinberg, & Bertsch, 1992). Each of these steps involves a distinct level of transcript analysis of the narrative, resulting in four unique voices of the subject: the first, the *plot voice* (the voice around what actually occurred); secondly, *the I voice* (how the subject places themselves within the story); and the third and fourth voices, the *contrapuntal voices* (the key differentiators and unique personal nuances). I poems were a means of extracting, from the second voice (the *I voice*), all the uses of *I* pronouns, during the narrative, and the associated verb with those *I* pronouns. The following I poem, from the doctoral study with senior Human Resource leaders (Maslak, 2008, p. 180) described this individual's reflection of self as a member of the SMT.

Jocelyn:
I'm a business partner,
I say yes,
I complement,
I am lucky
I just speak my truth.
I always have something to say,
I do things with purpose,
I "speak into the listening",
I learned.
I speak their language,
I listen for four things,
I talk about "human capital",
I mean,
I anticipate the question.
I kinda know
I don't know.
I gotta have a view,
I think,
I welcome the merits,
I'm always dying on every hill,
I need to learn.
I now hold people accountable,
I'm hands off,
I'm helpful,
I'm visible,
I send back emails with questions,
I'm approachable.
I want
I dream
I need
I'd rather "under promise and over deliver"
I'll be happy to help,
I've wanted to be in HR since age 16.

Contrast Jocelyn's experience of self, as a member of the SMT, with another participant, Donna (Maslak, 2008). While Jocelyn described herself as someone who has learned how she can best bring value to her place on the SMT and gain credibility through asking the right questions, learning to speak the other members' language, and being an active listener, Donna grew into a level of confidence with her place on the SMT. She knows what she needs to do to be accepted and to bring credibility to her position, yet it is a voice that is more resigned to *fitting in* than it is to *standing out*.

Donna:
I lead.
I never knew,
I now know,
I think,
I care.
I've proven,
I engage,
I don't attach,
I play the game.
I learn,
I listen,
I take notes,
I walk away,
I will follow.
I think out loud,
I come to conclusions,
I don't really mind,
I sit on the fence,
I say what I have to say,

I'm point accountable.
I learn,
I'm a team player,
I pray,
I believe,
I manage the white space,
I pick my time,
I'm not a big voice,
I will deliver.
I'm direct,
I'm credible
I'm prepared,
I'll make a decision,
I am
I know
I'm bold
I respect,
I've been heard.

(Maslak, 2008, p. 178)

For women leaders, the use of the I poem offers an opportunity to hear back, through the *language of poetry*, what messages of content, process and impact they are actually communicating when they speak. Offering leaders an opportunity to hear their own narrative, through a written transcript, and then in a summary of the *I voice*, provides women with insight into their authentic *whole voice*. By contrasting the I poem with the facial and body gestures of presence, an observer to the narrative is able to provide the leader with poignant feedback around specific dimension of voice that they can further enhance (i.e. specific words to say, pace, tone, pitch, use of vocal interferences) and how to maximize their physical stance, and gestures to reinforce their messages with clarity, deliberate intention and high impact. The 12 leaders from the doctoral study *The Senior Human Resource Leader as a Strategic Business Partner: A Story of Voice* (Maslak 2008), all found the I poem to be enlightening, especially to what the listener captured through their I voice, behind the narrative, when describing their participation as active members of their respective SMT. Many were unaware of the various dimensions of their voice, such as the pace they used, the distracting vocal interferences (i.e. uses of *ums, ers, you know,* etc), the pitch of their voice, the specific memorable or descriptive phrases used to describe various concepts, or the types of gestures or eye contact that they were naturally comfortable demonstrating (Verderber & Verderber, 2005).

The participants of the doctoral study also gained insight as to how the content and process elements of voice reflected one or more of the *Five Ways of Knowing* (Received Knowing, Subjective Knowing, Procedural Knowing, Silence, and Constructed Knowing), as described by Belenky, Clinchy, Goldberger, and Tarule (1997) as cited in Maslak, 2008. This is another area that is of benefit to women leaders. These ways of knowing were built on the original research that Gilligan (1982) started with understanding the experiences of developing women (Belenky et al., 1997). Their original research, from 1986, looked for common areas of knowledge among all women, regardless of background, that helped young developing girls understand what it means to be a woman, who they are, and how they are learn their place in the larger world especially in making decisions (Belenky et al., 1997). This earlier research resulted in five key knowledge dimensions that captured "some of the major ways women (regardless of class, race, or ethnic background) think about themselves, authorities, truth and life options (as cited in Goldberger, Tarule, Clinchy & Belenky, 1996, p. 4). They believed that *Silence* for women was linked directly with a loss of voice, mind and power from a state of not knowing. *Received* knowing was connected to those who learned from and deferred to powerful experts to teach them what they needed to know. *Subjective* knowing was personal, private, from the inner core of one's being where knowledge was based on intuition and feeling based versus logic and data driven. *Procedural* knowing developed through knowledge learned from specific scientific or logical processes of collecting, testing, and determining tangible value of claims, ideas and theories. *Constructed* knowledge developed from an understanding that there is more than one truth at play; multiple truths or approaches may be warranted depending on the situation, or context. In this type of knowing the idea involves "bringing the self and personal commitment into the center of the knowing process" (Goldberger et al., 1996, p. 5). Subsequent research on these *five ways of knowing*, focused on the application of the ways of knowing to specific professions, cultures, and communities and to collective action processes, but still concentrated only on the voices of women, a continued limitation of this research (Goldberger et al, 1996). Application of these ways of knowing was applied to all participants, including four males (Maslak, 2008). Findings from the Maslak 2008 study extended this comparison to include the four male participants interviewed. Three of the four male Senior Human Resource leaders' narrative analysis indicated a preference for *Procedural* knowing, and one more aligned with *Constructed* knowing. While not a large enough sample to generalize findings for all males, this was an attempt to highlight the various types of knowing associated with male voices. To understand a reference to the *ways of knowing*, consider and contrast the following three I poems.

Corinne:

I am woman
I'm mature
I listen
I read, I ask
I think (critically),
I reflect
I watch,
I learn.

I'm established,
I withdrew,
I fought back,
I guide,
I lead,
I serve.

I never give an answer,
I dig deeper,

I ask lots,
I choose carefully,
I'm deliberate,
I'm logical
I make decisions with information.

I care,
I intuit,
I know better,
I'm educated.

I'm lonely,
I envy,
I adapt,
I need,
I'm satisfied,
I lead.

Janice:

I know,
I am credible
I am...

I listen,
I try,
I think,
I learned,
I'm not invited.

I send,

I phone,
I tell,
I bring,
I'm collaborative,
I play team.

I ask,
I convince,
I walk the line
I sit,
I watch,
I wait.

Mark:

I'm a speaker,
I am fortunate,
I'm a decent listener,
I am sensitive,
I'm tactful.

I respect,
I am proud,
I try,
I am visionary.

I'm hard to read,
I control my emotions,
I have a poker face,
I'm a problem-solver.

I speak the language,
I express,
I reflect,
I'm on the outside looking in.

I test waters,
I lean,
I influence,
I choose my words carefully,
I check and validate
I'm new.

I'm sensitive,
I care,
I play team,
I want,
I'm patient.

I process,
I think,
I keep score,
I compete
I achieve.

I empower
I'm results-focused
I want to add real value,
I'm involved
I'm curious.

I push
I take pride
I believe
I inspire
I'm blessed.

Corinne speaks from a *Constructed* way of knowing, through the analysis of her full transcript, and this is reinforced in her I poem when she notes she "thinks critically . . . never gives an answer, I dig deeper, I ask lots" (Maslak, 2008, p. 177). Throughout her interview she is very reflective with each question, pausing and being very deliberate with her answers and choice of words. Janice's I poem, and analysis of her full transcript, is more reflective of the *Received* way of knowing. She uses silence to assess where others are coming from and she waits to be called upon, acting in deference to others with more authority or power than she perceives she holds (Maslak, 2008). Mark's I poem (Maslak, 2008, p. 178) noted a *Procedural* way of knowing, depicting a selfless approach to knowledge "yearn[ing] for a voice that is more integrated, individual, and original–a voice of their own" (Belenky et al., 1997, p. 124) and, throughout his interview transcript, stated he routinely uses silence for processing and thinking before he formulates a response.

How does one assess for effectiveness of voice, especially those women in positions of strong influence or whose voices are part of the decision making and strategic conversations? Ives (2005) found 31 factors that contributed to managers' decision to speak up or remain silent under controversial work situations. Of the 31 factors Ives described, the doctoral study confirmed that age and level of experience were key factors in the effectiveness of their voice (contributory to perceived level of credibility and expert power, as described by French and Raven (1959); followed closely by three additional factors, understanding the culture (its norms and common behaviors) of the respective SMT, the ability to speak that team's language, and the ability to speak the language of the associated business. Additional factors identified (beyond the 31 Ives found) were: an ability to link the language to the business strategy; the intentional choice of words; listening to understand other's perspectives; quality questions; personality preferences; level of preparedness; appropriate injection of humor; opportunity to educate; reliance on e-mail communication; sensitivity to others; expectations of the Chief Operating Officer / President; comfort with speaking, having a critical eye; sincerity and authenticity;

common sense; grace; poise; and positivity. Effectiveness of voice, relates to an individual's ability to clearly communicate their message so that others will receive, interpret and respond in a reciprocal manner to that message. The ability to know which words, which combinations of words, and how to inject the proper vocal intonations of tone, pitch, pace and clarity of speech is the art form of voice. Senge, Scharmer, Jaworski, and Flowers (2004) noted the concept of *presence* from the perspective of "deep listening–of being open beyond one's preconceptions and historical ways of making sense . . . leading to a state of "letting it come, of consciously participants in a larger field of change" (p. 11).

Madeline Albright (2003), in her memoirs, noted a key strategy she developed at the international table to find voice amongst the many male dominated voices. She referred to this strategy as *active interruption* and it was most effective when she could find the key moment to interject into the conversation a powerfully scripted message, with such conviction that it would bring an instant moment of reflection. She talks in her book, of how she not only learned to master this technique; but more importantly was respected for it by her male counterparts, regardless of the languages being spoken or the height of intensity of the conversation. Like her described heroes, Eleanor Roosevelt, Mahatma Gandhi, and Aung San Suu Kyi of Myanmar, she aspired to have a presence that commanded (not demanded) respect, and to whom people would listen willingly. "Warren Christopher had his elegant neckties; I had my pins or brooches . . . and each brooch reminded me that I am "first and foremost . . . a woman, and second Madame Secretary" (Albright, 2003, p. 343). While science may describe the mechanisms behind the control of breath and resonance / vibration produced to create sound that others can hear, knowing how to effectively use the physiological and insert intuition, emotion, poetry, objects of symbolism, into one's knowledge of language and voice, is the true art.

Tolbert and Hanafin (2006) referred to presence as "the translation of personal appearance, manner, values, knowledge, reputation, and other characteristics into interest and impact . . . Presence is the use of self with intent" (p. 72). Each person's presence is therefore unique, and their awareness of their specific presence may be at different levels of consciousness, reflective of the *past, present* or *future*. *Past* presence reflects characteristics of reputation, credibility and authority. *Present* presence deals with physical attributes of attire, posture, tone of voice, content of dialogue, gender, race, and ethnic affiliation. *Future* presence leans towards predictive actions beyond the here and now, invoking willingness for continued relationship in to the future. Tolbert and Hanafin go on to explain six ways to enhance awareness of presence for leaders. Denning (2007, p. 31) described six *enablers* that promoted the effectiveness of the language of leadership. These six include: the articulation of a clear and inspiring idea including any well-defined priorities; a commitment to change through a compelling leader story; an ability to understand the audience's story and see possibilities beyond what they might have seen; how to use *narrative intelligence* in storytelling; telling truthful stories that provide a message or key example; and deploying body language that is congruent with one's values and voice. A final I poem reflects my own awareness of presence, throughout the research and how conducting this study helped me become a far better woman leader by better understanding my own personal voice (Maslak, 2008, pp. 156–158).

Laurie:
I noted,
I assumed,
I had no difficulty
They called me.
I conducted
I made notes
I listened,
I believed,
Now I see...
I used the opportunity,
I assigned,
I extended,
I continued,
I sent,
I received,
I analyzed,
I maintained confidentiality,
I acknowledged,
I believed,
I possessed,
I realized,
I was most interested in "understanding".
I shared,
I focused,
I didn't need to speak,
I feel privileged and honored,
I must admit,
I attempted to honor,
So I could fully capture their voice.
I was reluctant to try
I became consciously aware
I was curious
I proposed,
I was told stories,
I wasn't entirely sure.
I use my own voice,
I have often used,
I conduct,
I create,
I capture,
I include,
I observe,
I ask myself,
I endeavored to convey their actual voice.
I attempt,
I perceive,
I look for,
I uncover,
I note,
I'm very conscious.
I speak,
I spend time with others,
I am a Senior HR leader,
I have hope.

(Maslak, 2008, pp. 156–158)

Conclusion

Linklater (1976, 1992) and Halpern and Lubar (2003) described the intense process, training, and discipline that actors undertake to prepare their voices and body actions for the stage (and film), and they advocated that great leaders should do the same; for

> leadership is not just a performing art, it may be the greatest performing art of all the only one that creates institutions of lasting value, institutions that can endure long after the stars who envisioned them have left the theatre. (Halpern & Lubar, 2003, p. xiii)

For females in leadership roles, inside or outside the workplace, the knowledge and use of the authentic personal voice is compelling for conveying confidence and a sense of personal power as a leader (Biggart & Hamilton, 1984). This personal power includes structure, the presence of authority, and human relations skill in understanding and influencing organizational processes. Each leader can learn, through reflective techniques, such as the I poem, the essence of their voice through their words, pace, tone, clarity of message, non-verbals, vocal interferences, and how to enhance their message in powerful ways (Denning, 2007; Tannen, 1994). This form of reflection takes women back to the *language of poetry* - a more intentional act of communication versus only a tool to deliver a message (Linklater, 1992; Halpern, & Lubar, 2003).

There is shift occurring, from hierarchical and bureaucratic structures in organizations where power inequities between genders continue (Witz & Savage, 1992), to new web-like structures, proposed by Helgesen (1990). In these new structures, authority is not from the head, but the heart, and does not rely on positional ranking to reinforce power; where the exchange of information and knowledge does not lessen authority in the web, rather it is strengthened; and one that facilitates leading from the center than at the top, for those who prefer to build consensus over issuing orders, and who do not need symbolic perks to define success in the hierarchy. In this new structure for organizations, the voice of the female leader needs to be able to reflect both genders (the masculine and the feminine) with confidence, grace and poise. This comes through discipline and training and development of the art. The Maslak (2008) study was the beginning of an attempt to highlight the authentic personal voice of each of the 12 Senior Human Resource leaders, as members of their respective SMT. While the results cannot be generalized for all senior or women leaders, its approach and methodology can and have been used repeatedly to assist individuals in uncovering, or learning for the first time, the messages they convey through the choice of words, the way they deliver their message, and the potential or actual impact of those messages on others. This is a gift to women leaders; an opportunity for females to be trained and to develop a discipline in how to use their voice *in service* of their vision and mission as leaders.

THOUGHTS FROM THE ACADEMIC ENTREPRENEUR

The problem to be solved:

- How to build capacity for the development of a female leader's *whole voice* and powerful leadership presence: an art or a science?

The goals:

- Providing a replicable technique that provides a reflection of a leader's authentic voice from the dimensions of content, process and impact.

- Enhanced awareness and continued development of one's "whole voice" and leadership presence as a defined leadership skill.
- Providing a means by which coaches and consultants can better reinforce a leader's ability to convey powerful messages through both words and demonstrated actions.

The questions to ask:

- What is the power behind *whole voice* for female leaders?
- What can women learn about their own voice that helps them be better leaders in all aspects of their lives (i.e. as wives, mothers, daughters, mentors, etc.)
- How can the use of the feminine voice in a historically masculine environment be a strong benefit to that culture?

Today's Business Application:

- Effective leaders who know and are intentional regarding the choice of their *whole voice and leadership presence* in all forms of communication.
- To enhance leadership development and coaching programs for leaders to train their voice and develop their leadership presence with others.
- Knowing the impact of cultural dimension influences on the choice of voice the leader conveys that is either in alignment with or contrary to that defined culture.

REFERENCES

Albright, M. (2003). *Madame Secretary: A memoir*. New York, NY: Miramax Books.

Aldoory, L. (1998). The language of leadership for female public relations professionals. *Journal of Public Relations Research, 10*(2), 73–80. http://dx.doi.org/10.1207/51532754xjprr1002_01

Belenky, M. F., Clinchy, B. M., Goldberger, N. R., & Tarule, J. M. (1997). *Women's ways of knowing: The development of self, voice, and mind (Reprint)*. New York, NY: Basic Books.

Biggart, N. W., & Hamilton, G. G. (1984). The power of disobedience. *Administrative Science Quarterly, 29,* 540–549. http://dx.doi.org/10.2307/2392938

Charlesworth, J. L. E. (2005). *No turning back: A phenomenological inquiry into women's experiences*. (Doctoral dissertation). Available from the University of Victoria Digital Database https://dspace.library.uvic.ca/handle/1828/636

Clarke, B., & Crossland, R. (2002). *The leader's voice: How your communication can inspire action and get results!* New York, NY: Peters Press and Select Books.

Denning, S. (2007). *The secret language of leadership: How leaders inspire action through narrative*. San Francisco, CA: Wiley & Sons.

Detert, J. R., & Burris, E. R. (2007). Leadership behavior and employee voice: Is the door really open? *Academy of Management Journal, 50,* 869–894. http://dx/doi.org/10.5465/amj.2007.26279183

Eagly, A. H., & Carli, L. L. (2007, September). Women and the labyrinth of leadership. *Harvard Business Review*, 2–10. Retrieved from https://hbr.org

French, R.P., Jr., & Raven, B. (1959). The bases of social power. In D.P. Cartwright (Ed.), *Studies in social power* (pp. 150–67). Ann Arbor, MI: University of Michigan Institute for Social Research.

Gilligan, C. (1982). *In a different voice: Psychological theory and women's development*. Cambridge, MA: Harvard University Press.

Gilligan, C. (1993). *In a different voice: Psychological theory and women's development* (Revised). Cambridge, MA: Harvard University Press.

Gilligan, C., Spencer, R., Weinberg, K., & Bertsch, T. (2003). On the listening guide: A voice-centered relational method. In Paul M. Camic, Jean E. Rhodes & Lucy Yardley (Eds.), *Qualitative research in Psychology: Expanding Perspectives in Methodology and Design*, 2–31. Washington, DC: American Psychological Association Press.

Goldberger, N., Tarule, J., Clinchy, B., & Belenky, M. (1996). *Knowledge, difference, and power: Essays inspired by women's ways of knowing.* (Eds.) New York, NY: Basic Books.

Halpern, B. L., & Lubar, K. (2003). *Leadership presence: Dramatic techniques to reach out, motivate, and inspire.* New York, NY: Gotham Books.

Hambrick, D. C. (2007). Upper echelons theory: An update (Editor's Forum). *Academy of Management Review, 32,* 334–343. http://dx.doi.org/10.5465.amr.2007.24345254

Hambrick, D. C., & Mason, P. A. (1984). Upper echelons: The organization as a reflection of its top managers. *Academy of Management Review, 9,* 193–206. http://dx.doi.org/10.2307/258434

Helgesen, S. (1990). *The female advantage: Women's ways of leadership.* New York, NY: Currency Doubleday.

Ives, C. M. (2005, December). *How do managers experience and make sense of their differential presence of voice in the workplace?* (Doctoral dissertation) Retrieved from ProQuest Dissertations and Theses database.

Linklater, K. (1976). *Freeing the natural voice.* New York, NY: Drama Book Specialists.

Linklater, K. (1992). *Freeing Shakespeare's voice: The Actor's guide to talking the text.* New York, NY: Theatre Communications Group.

Maslak, L. (2008). *The senior human resource leader as a strategic business partner: A story of voice* (Doctoral dissertation). Retrieved from from ProQuest Dissertations and Theses database. (UMI No. 3339022)

Senge, P., Scharmer, C. O., Jaworksi, J., & Flowers, B. S. (2004). *Presence: Human purpose and the field of the future.* Boston, MA: The Society for Organizational Learning.

Tannen, D. (1994). *Talking from 9 to 5: How women's and men's conversational styles affect who gets heard, who gets credit, and what gets done.* New York, NY: Morrow & Co.

Tolbert, M A. R., & Hanafin, J. (2006). Use of self in OD consulting: What matters is presence (Chapter Four, Part II) in B.B. Jones, &M. Brazzel (Eds), *The NTL Handbook of organizational development and change: principles, practices, and perspectives.* New York, NY: Pfeiffer.

Verderber, R. F., & Verderber, K. S. (2005). *Communicate!* (11th ed.). Belmont, CA: Thomson Wadsworth.

Walters, M. (2005). *Feminism: A very short introduction.* Oxford, UK: Oxford University Press.

Wheatley, M. J. (2002). *Turning to one another: Simple conversations to restore hope to the future.* San Francisco, CA: Berrett-Koehler.

Wheatley, M. J. (2007). *Finding our way: Leadership for uncertain times.* (Reprint). San Francisco, CA: Berrett-Koehler.

Whitney, D., & Trosten-Bloom, A. (2003). *The power of appreciative inquiry: A practical guide to positive change.* San Francisco, CA: Berrett-Koehler.

Witz, A., & Savage, M. (1992). Theoretical introduction: The gender of organizations. In A. Witz, & M. Savage (Eds.), *Gender bureaucracy,* Oxford: Blackwell Publishers.

Wylie, M. S. (2004). The untold story: Carol Gilligan on recapturing the lost voice of pleasure. *Psychotherapy Networker.* Retrieved from http://www.psychotherapynetworker.org

About the Author...

Dr. Laurie Maslak resides in Calgary, Alberta, Canada. Dr. Laurie holds several accredited degrees; a Bachelor of Nursing (BN) from the University of Calgary; a Master of Arts in Leadership and Training, from Royal Roads University; and a Doctorate of Philosophy in Organization and Management with a specialization in Leadership from Capella University. Her doctoral study is titled *The Senior Human Resource Leader as a Strategic Business Partner: A Story of Voice (2008)*.

Dr. Laurie is a well-respected facilitator, consultant, and educator. She has over 25 years of combined leadership, consulting and teaching experience in both the public and corporate business sectors. She is an Associate Consultant with DEKRA specializing in the areas of designing, reinforcing, and coaching strong organizational safety cultures and safety leadership development across North America.

Dr. Laurie is also President and Principal Consultant with Maslak & Associates Inc. Focused on enhanced team development and alignment, as well as strategic HR consulting. Laurie received the Human Resource Association of Calgary-Award of Excellence in 2002 and 2009. She has previously taught at the University of Calgary, Royal Roads University and Mount Royal University and is a regular conference speaker locally and nationally.

To reach Dr. Laurie L. Maslak for information on consulting or doctoral coaching, please e-mail: laurie.maslak@shaw.ca

10

The Paradox of Color Coding Leadership: Pink for Girls and Blue for Boys?

Dr. Aaron Glassman & Dr. Cheryl Lentz

Leadership presents a paradox as one tries to explain the evolution of its genesis. The fundamental question is to understand where the leadership story begins to attempt understanding of the application of leadership and of how leadership continues to evolve. When one examines the more than 65 different definitions of leadership, the question of gender emerges. Is there really a color to leadership? Does leadership come in pink for girls and blue for boys? Can society move toward a gender neutral yardstick in which to measure the quality and effectiveness of leadership independent of physicality? Although the thought of gender used to bring forth the concept of discrete gender identities, the literature suggests that gender is more of a spectrum beyond the labels and traditional stereotypes of what the titles male and female suggest. The purpose of this discussion is to examine the paradox of the color coding of leadership as culture continues to evolve into a universal definition and application of leadership independent of demographics (gender, ethnicity, national origin, or age) and to suggest that leadership and gender in particular be disconnected from the conversation.

To achieve these goals, this writing explores the existing leadership literature in an effort to determine what role, if any, gender plays in leadership in 2016 and moving forward. Existing leadership theories are dissected for gender reference or gender bias to determine the significance of gender among those theories, particularly linked to the focus of this volume, women in leadership. The preliminary goal is to isolate which theories are gender specific and which theories are gender agnostic, while accounting for confounding factors. A confounding factor would likely exist if one were to label a military leadership handbook from the 1940s *male dominant,* yet authored at such a time when women did not serve as military officers, rendering the point moot. Appropriate context must be part of the conversation, as well as historical context. Additionally, the goal is to examine the influence of refractive thinking regarding what is next for the evolution of leadership; we suggest disconnecting leadership from the traditional correlation with gender.

Once we identify gender roles among the theories, a critical analysis of the leadership landscape in 2016 will be presented as it relates to gender. This analysis includes discussion of the concept of primacy regarding the relationship to learned leadership behaviors, whether or not gender-based leadership is actually a form of sloppy stereotyping (suggesting male and female are discrete labels), and the challenges of including gender in the leadership discussion. An argument exists as to whether or not leadership theories and practices benefit from gender distinctions or are actually harmed by such. Examples from the aviation industry, such as Crew Resource Management (CRM), an applied leadership concept, frames the discussion. This chapter concludes with why color coding leadership may simply be perpetuating an old stereotype: pink is for girls and blue is for boys. Our goal is not to diminish the value of gender studies, minimize the tragedy of gender discrimination, or suggest gender differences do not exist. We posit that over focusing on gender and leadership may actually be counterproductive to the elimination of gender barriers as many leadership textbooks simply perpetuate untrue gender stereotypes.

The Role of Gender in Leadership

Many different leadership theories exist that many scholars and experts say fall along gender lines. For example, participatory leadership can be viewed as a more feminine style, while authoritarian leadership includes a more masculine label (Castillo-Mayén & Montes-Berges, 2014). The following section includes a review of leadership through a gender-focused lens along with the benefits and drawbacks of using such a lens from which to view leadership.

Traditional Theories of Leadership

There are many different leadership theories and many are clustered around certain commonalities. The foundational model of contemporary leadership research includes the great man theory. This theory includes the assumption held by many that *leaders are born, not made,* traditionally referring to the male leader (Mascone, 2013). The implication of this model is that the leader shapes history, instead of history (or the situation) shaping and influencing the leader. The question to ask is how realistic this theory may be in shaping the leadership conversation in 2016. Landy and Conte (2011) asserted that only two options exist; one can either change one's leadership style to match the situation or change the situation to match one's leadership style. The biographies of leaders considered to be of substantial influence demonstrate that every successful leadership career is a combination of individual attributes and the circumstances in which the leaders find themselves (Landry & Conte, 2011).

Another popular leadership theory, *trait theory* from the 1950s, evolved from the behavioral science perspective of leadership and superseded the great man theories as the accepted foundation of leadership studies (Bass, 1990). The trait theorists focused on the attributes of the individual leader and not on the environment with the assumption that an individual with the right traits could lead effectively in any situation (Bass, 1990). While not gender specific, some traits have been loosely assigned a gender reference (e.g., agreeableness, impulsivity, etc.).

Situational leadership evolved from this foundation, with the intention to refine trait theory by focusing on specific organizational situations (Woodruff, 2007). The continued evolution in leadership research led to other contingency theories. As Landry and Conte (2011) noted, "Because the success of any given leadership tactic is contingent upon multiple factors or situations, a number of contingency theories take into account the role of the situation in the exercise of leadership" (p. 557). Hershey and Blanchard's (1969) situational leadership theories supported this notion of adaptability to the needs of the situation as may be required (as cited in Hershey, Blanchard, & Johnson, 2012).

Additionally, transactional leadership merits discussion as a theory that emphasized the benefits each side gained from the transaction with the focal point on the accomplishment of organizational goals (Bass, 1990). The environment, good or bad, was not as critical to the outcome, because the leader worked within the boundaries of the environment to accomplish the goals (Woodruff, 2007). Transformational leadership emanated from a base of transactional leadership (Fry, 2003) and added feelings with limited consideration of the ethical makeup of the leader (Kanungo, 2001). Subsequently, transformational leaders resonate with many as more revolutionary than transactional leaders as those who develop emotional relationships with followers (Bass, 1990; Fry, 2003; Kanungo, 2001).

New Approaches and Emerging Topics and Challenges in Leadership Research

Two newer approaches evolved to include the leader-member exchange (LMX) theory and authentic leadership theory. The

LMX theory "proposes that leaders adopt different behaviors with individual subordinates" (Landry & Conte, 2011, p. 567). Authentic leadership "refers to a leader's sincerity and genuineness, and it includes the ability to share one's true self in a way that inspires and motivates one's followers" (Landry & Content, 2011, p. 567). Two components of the newer approaches are emotional intelligence (Goleman, 1998) and behavioral integrity. Both of these attributes are essential traits for effective organizational leaders in today's flattened hierarchical structures (Woodruff, 2007). As Landry and Conte (2011) noted, "Changes in the workplace since the 1980s have been substantial, resulting in a very different work environment for leaders" (p. 583). Subsequently, leaders adjusted to these changes with variations in new strategies for more effective outcomes through increased reliance on personal wisdom, experience, and knowledge.

Behavioral integrity reflects self-regulation and motivation that are components of emotional intelligence (Goleman, 1998). Emotional intelligence includes the willingness to live by personal beliefs and to be held accountable for personal decisions (Cashman, 2003). These are currently considered some of personality traits required for any emerging leader. So does that statement suggest that we are going back to trait theory? As Landry and Conte (2011) stated, "Trait theory is making a comeback in the form of studies examining the relationship of Big 5 personality traits and leader effectiveness" (p. 583). Landry and Conte explained this newer approach, "This modern approach defines personality traits behaviorally, has a general consensus on the meaning of these personality traits, and considers them in the context of organizational and situational variables" (p. 583). As one may see, many of the traditional leadership theories (trait, situational, transactional, and transformational) continue to be components of the newer theories that emerge. Consequently, in 2016, the leadership landscape continues to shift and change as organizations become more globally influenced and focused making the process even more difficult to write the rules on effective leadership.

Benefits and Drawbacks of Gender in Leadership

There are certainly benefits to viewing leadership though a gender-based lens. However, drawbacks also exist. Although the use of gender to make presumptions about leadership ability may be inappropriate and inaccurate, one cannot ignore the innate nature of gender differences. These gender differences have been comprehensively studied in a multi-disciplinary setting such as psychology, neurology, anthropometry, physiology, and medicine to name a few. It is not the purpose of this chapter to suggest that gender differences do not exist. They do. The simple act of observing how different genders engage similar situations (e.g., solve conflict, interact with children, etc.) will identify some gender distinctions or commonalities worth acknowledging. Yet, one must ask if these commonalities or acknowledgments are predictors of individual leadership behavior and effectiveness within the organization or simply generalities, the same generalities that cause one to ask tall people if they play basketball because one assumes that by a mere physical characteristic that they are more likely to do so. The question to ask is how the gender of the individual correlates in any way to capability. The contention presented here is simply one of the law of primacy—that male dominance in the workplace simply came first, becoming the yardstick to measure everything that came after—to include the leadership paradox and the *think manager-think male* presumption put forth by Virginia Schein in 1973 (Schein, Mueller, Lituchy, & Liu, 1996). The concept of primacy and gender differences includes a history to early childhood where pink and blue are introduced as gender-specific colors (Weisgram, Fulcher, & Dinella, 2014), and so begins the shaping of culture-based gender differences.

While specific reasons exist to view gender differences in other disciplines, such as the need for medical doctors who focus on gender specific medicine, do these differences convey to leadership and leadership effectiveness? This writing makes a strong argument that this type of thinking may be nothing more than sloppy stereotyping, lacking antecedent conditions such as a clear understanding of gender, and even rise to the level of illegal behavior if misapplied. This section includes discussion of benefits and drawbacks of using gender as a lens from which to view leadership.

Benefits

The empirical literature suggests that, in fact, differences exist between men and women as it relates to leadership. While these differences likely amount to generalizations, they are still of use to the individual as a baseline because the literature overwhelmingly indicates that leaders change their style over time (Eisner, 2013).

Indicated in the literature is the challenge for self-awareness within the hiring process. Landy and Conte (2011) offered that for new hires "the candidate pool is gradually narrowed through *rejection* [italics added] decisions until a selection is made and individual is placed in a position" (p. 278). Isn't this curious that one is not *selected* but chosen because of other *de*selections? This application of hiring practices offers a unique opportunity for how one evaluates new hires, as well as performance on the job. As offered by Landy and Conte (2011), "This does not mean we need to predict every aspect of job performance accurately, but it does mean that we should at least be trying to predict the important aspects of performance" (p. 294). Therefore, the more a candidate knows about oneself the better that person likely is to reflect and develop over time based on their individual traits, skills, and leadership preferences.

Drawbacks–Lead to Discrimination

Using a demographic viewpoint to study a specific construct, such as gender, to which there is no specific *average woman* or *average man* can lead to intentional or unintentional discrimination (Nier & Gaertner, 2012). The presumption is that men or women behave based on a set of averages or frequently identified traits. While this presumption may be true at the statistical level or even anecdotally useful when making sweeping generalizations, but to apply these generalizations to a specific individual would amount to stereotyping. When stereotyping leads to unjust or prejudicial treatment, discrimination exists.

Title VII of the Civil Rights Act of 1964 states that an organization cannot discriminate based on race, color, sex, or ethnic origin. Yet an overwhelming number of confirmed cases exist of gender-based discrimination in the literature (e.g., pay disparity, glass ceilings, etc.). The purpose of this chapter is not to discuss all aspects of gender discrimination, but we argue strongly that continuing the gender and leadership discussion may actually contribute to gender discrimination. This relationship is best illustrated using the following example:

Research shows that women are more nurturing and less authoritative than men. Bob is looking to hire a construction supervisor for his downtown high-rise project. This project will receive substantial media attention so the site must always look orderly and well-choreographed. Therefore, Bob needs a supervisor who will be authoritative, well organized, and speak confidently in front of the media.

Using gender stereotypes, a man would be best suited for the job. How could a nurturing woman possibly manage a predominantly male workforce in an authoritative way with poise and confidence? Of course, this entire discussion operates on one faulty premise; that *woman* has a specific and singular definition and all women are defined by that definition and bundle of traits. The notion that leadership abilities can be gauged in this manner is simply incorrect, making this entire line of thinking unethical and potentially illegal. This is so because using gender stereotypes to frame one's thinking is in and of itself a form of discrimination. What Bob is looking for are a set of skills that anyone can possess. Bob is likely influenced by prejudicial thoughts that he may be completely unaware of but that may even be a result of taking a college course in leadership or reading a leadership textbook that includes a discussion of gender and leadership.

With this in mind, one must wonder if society can move its standards to a place where being gender blind is possible regarding leadership. Can one simply use a carpenter metaphor to simply choose the most effective leadership style independent of the person that yields the most effective approach i.e. tool in the toolbox independent of gender? Hershey and Blanchard's (1969) situational leadership posited this approach, where the *situation* demands the solution, not pink or blue leadership style. Results drive the needs of the situation to defend a particular leadership style (as cited in Hershey et al., 2012). Leadership demands flexibility, adaptability, experience, and wisdom to know which tool will lead to the most effective outcome most often—none of these characteristics correlate with gender.

The question to ask is how then has the perception of gender somehow become accepted practice for correlation with the leadership question? According to Jonsen, Manervski, and Schenider (2010), based on the work of Eagley et al. (2003), knowing that an individual is female or male is not a reliable indicator of that person's leadership style. What matters more is the beliefs or sex-role stereotypes, rather than gender per se (based on the work of Butterfield & Powerll, 1981; Yammarino et al., 1997). Ultimately, this research begs the question whether a leadership correlation to gender can truly be based on empirical findings, a construct based on subjective social perceptions, societal mechanisms, and cultural interpretations. In other words, researchers continue to ask the question whether an empirical connection exists between gender and leadership.

Drawbacks–Gender as a Spectrum (Antecedent Conditions)

One of the key arguments against studying gender and leadership is the presumption that gender falls into two discrete bins; male and female and that people in each bin share substantial commonalities (G.I. Joe and Barbie are often used, polarizing examples). Therefore, the notion of two discrete bins is an antecedent condition to any gender and leadership research. We argue in this writing that gender is a spectrum and the absence of two discrete bins means that gender and leadership cannot be effectively studied because one of the antecedent conditions, a clear and universal definition of gender, is absent. In the late 1990's, the scholarly literature saw a marked increase the use of the term gender nonconformity and the literature related to this topic has increased every year since. Meyer (2016) used references from multiple international legal doctrines to suggest that *woman* can be a biological, anatomical, genetic, gender performance, or a gender identity reference. This finding implies that gender is more than a binary discussion of pink and blue and that culture has a substantial influence on gender labeling.

In addition, the Lesbian, Bisexual, Gay, and Transgender (LBGT) community seems to embrace gender as a spectrum and Liberman and Golom (2015) suggested gender labeling in management is an additional source of discrimination. There are even scales used to measure gender nonconformity such as the Gender Role Conflict Scale that further suggest gender is anything but two discrete bins. Finally, even the most basic anecdotal evidence requires one to do nothing more than look around at others. What do a female drill sergeant and an effeminate male have in common? They both fall within the spectrum of gender and likely have different skill sets. Traditional male / female stereotypes simply fail to address the complexities of gender or explain their apparent differences. Furthermore, the literature suggests that gender definitions are socially constructed and they have a social influence. With a focus on globalization, the argument seems near impossible for a single, socially constructed definition of gender to be applicable to the myriad of cultures found within the United States and around the world. The World Health Organization (WHO) (2016) acknowledged this difficulty and suggested that gender distinctions will vary greatly from culture-to-culture. Therefore, one must wonder what good adding gender as a variable to the leadership discussion contributes at all. The U.S. Army recruited the first female drill instructor in in 1971 (U.S. Army, 2016). Her leadership skills are unquestionable. However, one must ask if she would more closely align with G.I. Joe figurines or Barbie dolls; polarizing gender stereotypes or arguably useless labels. We argue that *effective* is the most appropriate label regardless of gender and effective leadership is worthy of study.

Discussion

Numerous authors further the gender discussion by including gender when discussing leadership effectiveness, leadership traits, and follower expectations (Butterfield & Powell, 1981; Powell, 2011; Yammarino et al., 1997). There is also a body of research that attempts to catalog gender differences and relate those differences to leadership competencies. Although these alignments may exist in stereotypical form, we argue that even the definition of gender is more abstract than previously considered and the use of gender in reference to leadership may be in error. We further argue that one must step away from gender and ask what specific leadership competencies are needed based on follower responsiveness in a given circumstance, organization, or setting. In other words, we must view leadership as a gender agnostic construct to avoid further clouding how we identify successful leadership. Numerous studies affirmed this viewpoint that indicated: a) followers have no gender preference of their leaders; b) male and female leaders can be equally as effective; and, c) the behaviors of managers show no specific gender alignment.

Ultimately, the premise and concern for success in business is *results* driven, not *gender* driven. Pech and Durden (2004) argued, "many organizations fail because of weaknesses in the decision processes of their leaders" (p. 66). In this context, success or failure is because of *skill* and *mastery*, not gender. Thus, the concept of inclusiveness becomes crucial to consider because of everyone being of strategic importance in the organization; everyone's value remains a valid and plausible argument, crucial to the success of the organization (Lentz, 2007).

Gender Agnostic Examples

Eisner (2013) concluded that by the time one reaches the level of senior executive men and women show almost no performance-related differences. This lack of differentiation could be because of self-selection in that only people with certain traits apply for or promote into executive positions, or it could be a function of career evolution and an executive mindset. The same study indicated that male and female leaders evolve over time and change their leadership style supporting the claim that people, regardless of gender, can evolve effectively into senior leadership roles (Eisner, 2013). Regardless, Eisner's results seems to suggest a more gender agnostic view of senior leadership in the organizations studied. Growing evidence suggests that what is observed in the boardroom is inconsistent with the foundational theories presented in the literature. As this gap widens, an argument exists that the foundational literature may no longer be accurate, instead driven by role congruence theory; the notion that when one acts outside of their gender stereotype their effectiveness or alignment is judged as it relates to that stereotype not their actual effectiveness as a leader (Perrone, Webb, & Blalock, 2005).

Crew Resource Management (CRM), a concept used on the flight deck of every airliner, is an excellent example of gender agnostic leadership. CRM is a process to where crew train together in effective team behaviors (leadership and followership), team building that fosters crew effectiveness, proper communications, advocacy for an outcome (e.g., flight safety), stress management, situational awareness, problem-solving and decision-making, and doing so all while flying and managing the aircraft (Orlady, Orlady, & Lauber, 1999). The argument exists that CRM is effective because of the lack of consideration of individual traits and preferences over the needs of the aircraft. In other words, the aircraft wants to be flown a particular way, not caring who is doing the flying leaving race, gender, and other variables absent in the discussion of flight safety. After all, just about every airline in the world uses CRM, transcending all discussions of culture, race, ethnicity, gender, etc.

CRM has been so effective at enhancing flight safety and crew coordination that other industries continue to adopt its teachings. Pinsky, Taichman, and Sarment (2010) suggested ways to adapt CRM to dentistry. Bringelson and Pettitt (1995) discussed ways of applying CRM to emergency medicine, Gordon (2006) to nursing, Schwartz and Hobbs (2014) pharmacy operations, and Ricci and Brumsted (2012) operating room safety. Clearly, CRM permeated the healthcare industry because similar to aviation, health care can be a high-risk endeavor. What is most interesting is that CRM demonstrates broader applications to large groups of people, while still largely ignoring individual differences; remaining a highly effective, mission-driven leadership, and behavioral protocol.

In addition to healthcare, CRM practices have made their way to the offshore oil industry (Flin, 1997), the automotive industry (Marguardt, Robelski, & Hoeger, 2010), and other high-reliability industries (Flin, O'Connor & Mearns, 2002). The use of CRM may be attractive to so many industries because unlike nonspecific theories that are very individualistic, the CRM premise is somewhat task-oriented but in the absence of a specific task focuses on how to make decision and problem solve within a group setting. For those who may argue that senior leadership is less structured, CRM addresses decisions under conditions of uncertainty and even enables some degree of group creativity. The 'Miracle on the Hudson' where Captain Chesley Sullenberger landed a crippled Airbus A320 with no engine power on the Hudson River is a good example of effective CRM under extreme stress, time pressure, and ambiguity. No checklist existed for that action, but quality thinking and cohesive teamwork saved the lives of all onboard. We believe that is highly unlikely that any passenger aboard that aircraft expressed concern about the gender of the crew, only how that crew performed.

Recommendation: Disconnect Gender From the Leadership Conversation

Because of the arguments outlined within this chapter, the question asked becomes whether or not leadership and gender should be disconnected from the leadership conversation. Does leadership consider what bathroom one may use? Gender may offer the perception of correlation to leadership in the traditional sense of female vs. male labels, however are these labels as definitive as once thought? Can females not have masculine qualities and vice versa? While it is acknowledged that gender and sex differ, the leadership literature still uses these concepts interchangeably and fails to address the limitations of such labels.

Leadership as a Tool in a Carpenter's Toolbox

The argument proposed is that leadership is simply a gender neutral tool in a carpenter's toolbox. The goal is simply to use the most appropriate tool for the most appropriate outcome. One does not want to buy a hammer or the nail, as the goal is not even the nail in the wall—the outcome is the picture on the wall. Using an outcome based thinking, one asks the goal for leadership—to achieve a particular outcome. Does a gender-based conversation achieve this end?

Think of a specific job description such as a firefighter or a police officer or military standards. These standards are not pink for girls or blue for boys. The POSITION requires specific standards independent of gender. Either one can pick up the firehose and have physical conditioning to handle the demands of the job or they can't. Demographics such as gender should not be part of the conversation simply as a result of traditional stereotypes that are inaccurate and sloppy.

The evolution of leadership should focus on the individual and their capability to achieve a specific outcome. One should break the yardstick from the law of primacy to move to being *gender blind and discard gender stereotypes and simply focus on effective performance.*

Conclusion

The conclusion drawn with these arguments is that leadership presents a paradox as one tries to explain the evolution of its genesis. The fundamental question presented was to understand where the leadership story begins regarding the application of leadership and of how leadership continues to evolve. When one examines the more than 60+ different definitions of leadership, the question of gender emerges. Is there really a color to leadership? Does leadership come in pink for girls and blue for boys? While the thought of gender used to bring forth the concept of discrete gender identities, the literature suggested that gender is more of a spectrum beyond the labels and traditional stereotypes of what the titles male and female suggest. The purpose of this discussion was to examine the paradox of the color coding of leadership as culture evolves into a universal definition and application of leadership independent of demographics (gender, ethnicity, national origin, or age).

With all that is known about leadership and gender, we feel it is time to disconnect gender from leadership. Although gender is an important area of study, attempting to over-catalog leadership as it relates to race, gender, culture, or national origin may only serve to slow our understanding of leadership. Our goal is to make leadership opportunities accessible to everyone without concern if the individual fits a particular gender stereotype. This new viewpoint may free us from our own desire to overthink as one considers the refractive thinking perspective of what may lie ahead.

THOUGHTS FROM THE ACADEMIC ENTREPRENEUR

The problem to be solved:

- Is there really a color to leadership? Does leadership come in pink for girls and blue for boys?

The goals:

- More effective understanding of the physicality of gender, not related to leadership.
- Disconnecting gender from the leadership conversation.

The questions to ask:

- Does the gender question remain relevant in the business space?
- Is outcome more important than the gender identity of the person creating the change?

Today's Business Application:

- Disconnecting gender from the conversation accomplishes a more effective results driven outcome.
- Reframing leadership as simply *one who can lead* without prescriptive definition makes leadership more accessible to the organization regardless of individual labels.

REFERENCES

Bass, B. M. (1990). *Handbook of leadership: Theory, research, & managerial applications* (3rd ed.). New York, NY: The Free Press.

Bennis, W. G. (1959). Leadership theory and administrative behavior: The problem of authority. *Administrative Science Quarterly, 4*(3), 259–302. doi:10.2307/2390911

Bringelson, L. S., & Pettitt, M. A. (1995). Applying airline crew resource management in emergency medicine. *Human Factors and Ergonomics Society Annual Meeting Proceedings, 39*, 728–732. doi:10.1177/154193129503901103

Cashman, K. (2003). *Awakening the leader within*. Hoboken, NJ: Wiley and Sons.

Castillo-Mayn, R., & Montes-Berges, B. (2010). Analysis of current gender stereotypes. *Anales De Psicologa (Murcia, Spain), 30*(3), 1060. doi:10.1037/t42833–000

Collins, J. C. (2009). *How the mighty fall: And why some companies never give in*. New York, NY: HarperCollins.

Dobbins, G. H., & Platz, S. J. (1986). Sex differences in leadership: How real are they? *The Academy of Management Review, 11*, 118–127. doi:10.5465/amr.1986.4282639

Dineen, B. R., Lewicki, R. J., & Tomlinson, E. C. (2006, May). *Supervisory guidance and behavioral integrity: Relationships with employee citizenship and deviant behavior*. Journal of Applied Psychology, 91, 622–635. doi:10.1037/0021-9010.91.3.622

Eisner, S. (2013). Leadership: Gender and executive style. *SAM Advanced Management Journal, 78*(1), 26.

Embry, A., Padgett, M. Y., & Caldwell, C. B. (2008). Can leaders step outside of the gender box?: An examination of leadership and gender role stereotypes. *Journal of Leadership & Organizational Studies, 15*(1), 30–45. doi:10.1177/1548051808318412

Flin, R. H. (1997). Crew resource management for teams in the offshore oil industry. *Team Performance Management: An International Journal, 3*(2), 121–129. doi:10.1108/13527599710190876

Flin, R., O'Connor, P., & Mearns, K. (2002). Crew resource management: Improving team work in high reliability industries. *Team Performance Management: An International Journal, 8*(3/4), 68–78. doi:10.1108/13527590210433366

Fry, L. W. (2003). Toward a theory of spiritual leadership. *The Leadership Quarterly, 14*, 693–727. doi:10.1016/j.leaqua.2003.09.001

Goleman, D. (1998). *Working with Emotional Intelligence*. New York, NY: Bantam.

Gordon, S. (2006). Crew resource management. *Nursing Inquiry, 13*(3), 161–162. doi:10.1111/j.1440-1800.2006.00327.x

Harriman, A. (1996). *Women/men/management* (2nd ed.). Westport, CT: Praeger Publishers.

Hershey, P., Blanchard, K., & Johnson, D. E. (2012, July 28). *Management of organizational behavior* (10th ed.). Boston, MA: Pearson Education.

Johnson, S. K., Murphy, S. E., Zewdie, S., & Reichard, R. J. (2008). The strong, sensitive type: Effects of gender stereotypes and leadership prototypes on the evaluation of male and female leaders. *Organizational Behavior and Human Decision Processes, 106*(1), 39–60. doi:10.1016/j.obhdp.2007.12.002

Jonsen, K., Maznevski, M., & Schneide, S. C. (2010, September). Gender differences in leadership: Believing is seeing: Implications for managing diversity. *Equality, Diversity, and Inclusion: An International Journal, 29*, 549–572. doi:10.1108/02610151011067504

Kanungo, R. N. (2001). Ethical values of transactional and transformational leaders. *Canadian Journal of Administrative Sciences, 18*, 257–265. doi:10.1111/j.1936-4490.2001.tb00261.x

Landy, F. J., & Conte, J. M. (2010). *Work in the 2st century: An introduction to industrial and organizational psychology* (3rd ed.). Malden, MA: Blackwell Publishing.

Lentz, C. (2007). *Strategic decision-making in organizational performance: A quantitative study of employee inclusiveness* (Doctoral dissertation). Retrieved from ProQuest Dissertations and Theses database. (UMI No. 3277192)

Liberman, B. E., & Golom, F. D. (2015). Think manager, think male?: Heterosexuals' stereotypes of gay and lesbian managers. *Equality, Diversity and Inclusion: An International Journal, 34*, 566–578. doi:10.1108/EDI-01-2015-0005

Marquardt, N., Robelski, S., & Hoeger, R. (2010). Crew resource management training within the automotive industry: Does it work? *Human Factors: The Journal of Human Factors and Ergonomics Society, 52*(2), 308–315. doi:10.1177/0018720810366258

Mascone, C. F. (2013, August). Are leaders born or made? *Chemical Engineering Progress, 109*(8), 3. Retrieved from http://uopx.summon.serialssolutions.com.contentproxy.phoenix.edu/search?s.q=leaders+are+born%2c+not+made&s.fvf[]=IsScholarly,true&keep_r=true

Meyer, E. (2016). Designing women: The definition of "woman" in the convention on the elimination of all forms of discrimination against women. *Chicago Journal of International Law, 16*(2), 553.

Nier, J. A., & Gaertner, S. L. (2012). The challenge of detecting contemporary forms of discrimination. *Journal of Social Issues, 68*(2), 207–220. doi:10.1111/j.1540-4560.2012.01745.x

Orlady, H. W., Orlady, L. M., & Lauber, J. K. (1999). *Human factors in multicrew flight operations*. Brookfield, VT: Ashgate.

Osborn, R. N., & Vicars, W. M. (1976). Sex stereotypes: An artifact in leader behavior and subordinate satisfaction analysis? *The Academy of Management Journal, 19*, 439–449. doi:10.2307/255609

Pech, R., & Durden, G. (2004).Where the decision-makers went wrong: From capitalism to cannibalism. *Corporate Governance, 4*(1), 65. doi:10.1108/14720700410521970

Perrone, K. M., Webb, L. K., & Blalock, R. H. (2005). The effects of role congruence and role conflict on work, marital, and life satisfaction. *Journal of Career Development, 31*(4), 238; 238.

Pierce, J. L., & Newstrom, J. W. (2011). *Leaders and the leadership process: Building self-assessments and applications* (6th ed.). New York, NY: McGraw Hill.

Pinsky, H. M., Taichman, R. S., & Sarment, D. P. (2010). Adaptation of airline crew resource management principles to dentistry. *The Journal of the American Dental Association, 141*, 1010–1018. doi:10.14219/jada.archive.2010.0316

Powell, G. N. (2011). The gender and leadership wars. *Organizational Dynamics, 40*(1), 1–9. doi:10.1016/j.orgdyn.2010.10.009

Ricci, M. A., & Brumsted, J. R. (2012). Crew resource management: Using aviation techniques to improve operating room safety. *Aviation, Space, and Environmental Medicine, 83,* 441.

Rhee, K. S., & Sigler, T. H. (2015). Untangling the relationship between gender and leadership. *Gender in Management: An International Journal, 30*(2), 109–134. doi:10.1108/GM-09-2013-0114

Schein, V. E., Mueller, R., Lituchy, T., & Liu, J. (1996). Think manager—think male: A global phenomenon? *Journal of Organizational Behavior, 17*(1), 33–41. http://dx.doi.org/10.1002/(sici)1099-1379(199601)17:1<33::aid-job778>3.0.co;2-f

Shimanoff, S. B., & Jenkins, M. M. (1991). Leadership and gender: Challenging assumptions and recognizing resources. In R. S. Cathcart & L. A. Samovar (Eds.), *Small group communication: A reader* (6th ed., pp. 101–133). Dubuque, IA: W. C. Brown.

Schwartz, M. D., & Hobbs, W. H. (2014). Teaching aviation crew resource management in a pharmacy curriculum. *American Journal of Pharmaceutical Education, 78*(3), 66. http://dx.doi.org/10.5688/ajpe78366

Senge, P. (2006). *The fifth discipline: The art & practice of the learning organization* (Revised ed.). New York, NY: Doubleday / Currency.

Senge, P., Roberts, C., Ross, R., Smith, B., & Kleiner, A. (1994). *The fifth discipline fieldbook: Strategies for building a learning organization.* New York, NY: Currency Books.

Smith, S., (2014). Limitations to equality: Gender stereotypes and social change. *Juncture, 21*(2), 150.

U.S. Army. (2016). *History of the drill sergeant.* Retrieved from https://www.army.mil/drillsergeant/history.html

Wajcman, J. (1998). *Managing like a man: Women and men in corporate management.* University Park, PA: Pennsylvania State University Press.

Weisgram, E. S., Fulcher, M., & Dinella, L. M. (2014). Pink gives girls' permission: Exploring the roles of explicit gender labels and gender-typed colors on preschool children's toy preferences. *Journal of Applied Developmental Psychology, 35,* 401–409. doi:10.1016/j.appdev.2014.06.004

Woodruff, T. M. (2007). *Leadership, board governance, director independence, and corporate performance: A quantitative, correlational study of community banks.* (Doctoral dissertation). Retrieved from ProQuest Dissertations and Theses database. (UMI No. 3294998)

World Health Organization (WHO). (2016). *What do we mean by "sex" and "gender"?* Retrieved from http://apps.who.int/gender/whatisgender/en/

About the Authors...

Dr. Aaron M. Glassman holds several accredited degrees; a Bachelor of Science (BS) in Human Development from Empire State College; a Master of Aeronautical Science degree (MAS) with a specialization in Human Factors, and a Doctor of Management Degree (DM) from the University of Maryland University College. He is also an FAA Safety Team Representative and serves on numerous panels, committees, and serves on the editorial review board of the Enterprise Architecture Body of Knowledge (EABOK).

Dr. Aaron is an Assistant Professor in the College of Business at Embry-Riddle Aeronautical University. His interest in gender and leadership stems from his experience as a pilot, flight instructor, and aviation training business owner where he worked tirelessly to increase diversity in the pilot population. Dr. Aaron also works *pro bono* with numerous women and minority owned business as a business development and strategic planning coach. His overarching goals as both a scholar and practitioner are to help organizations reach their full potential and leverage the power of people.

To reach Dr. Aaron Glassman for research collaboration, speaking opportunities, or consulting projects please email him at aaron@draaronglassman.com

International best-selling author Dr. Cheryl A. Lentz, known as *The Academic Entrepreneur*, holds several accredited degrees; a Bachelor of Arts (BA) from University of Illinois, Urbana-Champaign; a Master of Science in International Relations (MSIR) from Troy University; and a Doctorate of Management (DM) in Organizational Leadership from the University of Phoenix School of Advanced Studies. She has her Sloan C Certification from Colorado State University–Global, as well as her Quality Matters Peer Reviewer (APP / PRC) Certification.

Dr. Cheryl, affectionately known as *Doc C* to her students, is a university professor on faculty with Embry-Riddle University, Grand Canyon University, University of Phoenix, The University of the Rockies, and Walden University. Dr. Cheryl serves as a dissertation mentor / chair and committee member. She is also a dissertation coach, offering expertise as a professional editor for APA style for graduate thesis and doctoral dissertations, as well as faculty journal publications and books.

Awards include: Walden Faculty of the Year, DBA Program, 2016; Walden Woods Exemplar; and the University of Phoenix Alumni Community Service Award 2012, as well as 16 writing awards.

Dr. Cheryl is also an active member of Alpha Sigma Alpha Sorority.

She is a prolific author with more than 30 publications known for her writings on *The Golden Palace Theory of Management* and refractive thinking. Additional published works include her dissertation: *Strategic Decision Making in Organizational Performance, Journey Outside the Golden Palace, The Consumer Learner, Technology That Tutors, Effective Study Skills,* International Best Seller: *The Expert Success Solution,* and contributions to the award winning series: *The Refractive Thinker®: Anthology of Doctoral Learners, Volumes I–XI.*

To reach Dr. Cheryl Lentz for information on refractive thinking, professional editing, consulting, or guest speaking, please visit her website: www.DrCherylLentz.com or her company website www.LentzLeadership.com or e-mail: drcheryllentz@gmail.com

Index

A
Academic mentoring, 21
AICPA Vision 2011 Project, 66
All but dissertation (ABD), 17, 21, 25

B
Business value, 50, 54, 55–57

C
Color coding, 153–154, 168
Collaboration, 54, 56, 75, 83, 85–86, 88–89
Communication, 11, 18, 19, 25, 32–33, 36, 42, 51, 54, 56, 62–65, 71, 86, 100–101, 103, 106, 108, 118–119, 122, 124, 131, 142, 146, 148, 165
Corporate social responsibility, 49, 52, 62, 68, 71

D
Dissertation writing process, 18, 20, 21–27

E
Emotional intelligence, 51, 55–56, 100, 118, 122, 124, 157
Employee turnover, 32, 35, 37
Empowerment, 37, 42, 44, 77, 95

F
Firm performance, 31–35, 37–44
Focus group, 49, 54–55, 135

G
Gender bias, 32, 34, 43–44, 95, 103, 105, 108, 154
Gender differences, 79, 95, 106, 154, 158, 159, 163
Gender equity, 122
Gender identities, 153, 168
Gender stereotypes, 103. 154, 160–161, 163
Gender, 58, 72, 82, 84, 95–96, 99, 102–106, 108, 120, 122, 124, 133, 144, 146, 153–156, 158–164, 166–169
Gendering, 5–6
Generation gender bias, 8
Glass ceiling, 3, 90, 97, 104–105, 107, 116–117, 160

H
Healthcare change, 115, 121, 124–125
Healthcare organizational change, 113–115, 123–125
Healthcare organizations, 113–114, 116, 121–125

I
Innovation, 32–43
I poem, 135–139, 141–142, 144, 146

K
Knowledge management, 31–44

L
Leadership development, 6, 78, 106, 148
Leadership paradox, 158
Leadership presence, 134, 147–148

M
Mentor mentee relationship, 19, 21, 23–27
Mentor, 1–4, 6–8, 18–27
Mentoring female doctoral students, 20–21
Mentoring women, 17, 20, 26, 75, 82, 84, 86–87, 89
Mentoring, 1–4, 9–12, 17, 19–26
Motivation, 2–4, 11–12, 51–52, 55–56, 68

N
Native American, 49–52, 56–58
Networking, 70–72, 75–76, 80–81, 83, 85, 88–90

O
Organizational culture, 4–5, 12, 35, 37, 42, 44, 100, 105

P
Personal power, 134, 146
Philanthropic opportunity, 55
Power, 131–135, 139–140, 142–143, 146–148, 162, 166
The Patient Protection and Affordable Care Act (PPACA), 113–115, 121, 123

R
Resilience, 55, 56, 89, 118

S
Science, Technology, Engineering, and Math (STEM), 75, 84, 89
Ship repair, 32–32, 39, 41, 43
Situational leadership theory, 49
Social networks, 7
Soft skills, 100
Strategic vision, 51, 54, 56, 78
Success, 9–10, 19–20, 32, 41, 50, 68, 75–77, 81–83, 85–88

T
Tribal gaming, 49–51–53, 55, 57

U
U.S. Navy, 31

V
Voice, 131–139, 142–148

W
Women in educational leadership, 17, 20, 27, 82, 84

The Refractive Thinker®
AND
Pensiero Press

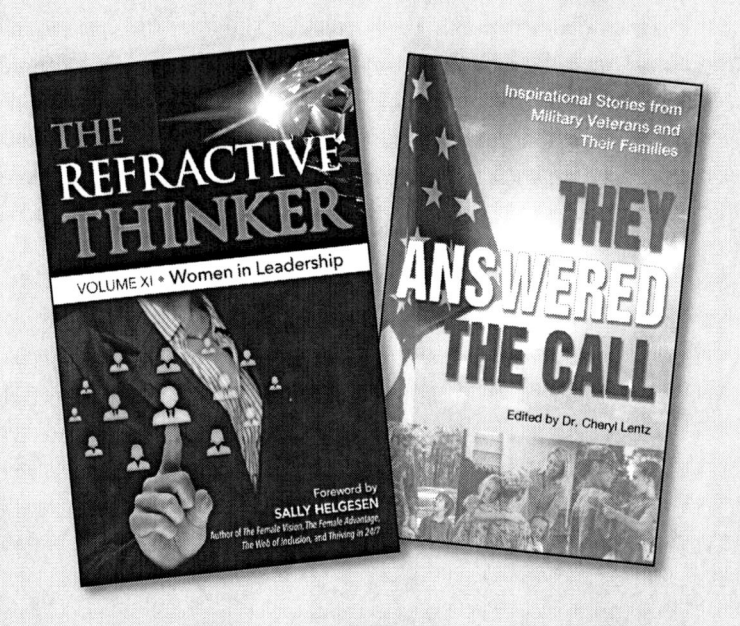

2016–2017 CATALOG

The Refractive Thinker®:
An Anthology of Higher Learning

The Refractive Thinker® Press
7124 Glyndon Trail NW
Albuquerque, NM 87114 USA

www.RefractiveThinker.com
blog: www.DissertationPublishing.com

*Individual authors own the copyright to their individual materials. The Refractive Thinker® Press has each author's permission to reprint.

Books are available through The Refractive Thinker® Press at special discounts for bulk purchases for the purpose of sales promotion, seminar attendance, or educational purposes. Special volumes can be created for specific purposes and to organizational specifications. Orders placed on www.RefractiveThinker.com for students and military receive a 15% discount. Please contact us for further details.

Refractive Thinker® logo by Joey Root; The Refractive Thinker® Press logo design by Jacqueline Teng, cover design by Peri Poloni-Gabriel, Knockout Design (knockoutbooks.com), cover design & production by Gary A. Rosenberg (thebookcouple.com).

Pensiero Press

Pensiero Press
7124 Glyndon Trail NW
Albuquerque, NM 87114 USA
www.ThePensieroPress.com

> I *think* therefore I am.
> —Renee Descartes

> I *critically think* to be.
> I *refractively think* to change the world.

Thank you for joining us as we continue to celebrate the accomplishments of doctoral scholars affiliated with many phenomenal institutions of higher learning. The purpose of the anthology series is to share a glimpse into the scholarly works of participating authors on various subjects.

The Refractive Thinker® serves the tenets of leadership, which is not simply a concept outside of the self, but comes from within, defining our very essence; where the search to define leadership becomes our personal journey, not yet a finite destination.

The Refractive Thinker® is an intimate expression of who we are: the ability to think beyond the traditional boundaries of thinking and critical thinking. Instead of mere reflection and evaluation, one challenges the very boundaries of the constructs itself. If thinking is *inside* the box, and critical thinking is *outside* the box, we add the next step of refractive thinking, *beyond* the box. Perhaps the need exists to dissolve the box completely. The authors within these pages are on a mission to change the world. They are never satisfied or quite content with *what is* or asking *why*, instead these authors intentionally strive to push and test the limits to ask *why not*.

We look forward to your interest in discussing future opportunities. Let our collection of authors continue the journey initiated with Volume I, to which *The Refractive Thinker*® will serve as our guide to future volumes. Come join us in our quest to be refractive thinkers and add your wisdom to the collective. We look forward to your stories.

Please contact The Refractive Thinker® Press for information regarding these authors and the works contained within these pages. Perhaps you or your organization may be looking for an author's expertise to incorporate as part of your annual corporate meetings as a keynote or guest speaker(s), perhaps to offer individual, or group seminars or coaching, or require their expertise as consultants.

Join us on our continuing adventures of *The Refractive Thinker®* where we expand the discussion specifically begun in Volume I, Leadership; Volume II (Editions 1–3), Research Methodology; Volume III, Change Management; Volume IV, Ethics, Leadership, and Globalization; Volume V, Strategy in Innovation; Volume VI, Post-Secondary Education; Volume VII, Social Responsibility; Volume VIII, Effective Business Practices in Motivation & Communication; Volume IX, Effective Business Practices in Leadership & Emerging Technologies; Volume X, Effective Business Strategies for the Defense Industry Sector; and Volume XI, Women in Leadership. All our volumes are themed to explore the realm of strategic thought, creativity, and innovation.

Dr. Cheryl A. Lentz, managing editor of The Lentz Leadership Institute, explains the unique benefits of the books for readers:

"They celebrate the diffusion of innovative refractive thinking through the writings of these doctoral scholars as they dare to think differently in search of new applications and understandings of research. Unlike most academic books that merely define research, The Refractive Thinker® offers unique applications of research from the perspective of multiple authors—each offering a chapter based on their specific expertise."

Books from
THE REFRACTIVE THINKER® PRESS

The Refractive Thinker® Series

Volume I: An Anthology of Higher Learning

Volume II, 1st through 3rd Editions: Research Methodology

Volume III: Change Management

Volume IV: Ethics, Leadership, and Globalization

Volume V: Strategy in Innovation

Volume VI: Post-Secondary Education

Volume VII: Social Responsibility

Volume VIII: Effective Business Practices for Motivation and Communication

Volume IX: Effective Business Practices in Leadership & Emerging Technologies

Volume X: Effective Business Strategies for the Defense Industry Sector

Volume XI: Women in Leadership

Refractive Thinker volumes are available in e-book, Kindle®, iPad®, Nook®, and Sony Reader™, as well as individual e-chapters by author.

COMING SOON!
The Refractive Thinker®: Volume XII: Cybersecurity

Telephone orders: Call us at 702.719.9214

Website orders: Please place orders through our website:
www.RefractiveThinker.com

Postal Orders: The Refractive Thinker® Press
7124 Glyndon Trail NW
Albuquerque, NM 87114 USA

Coming Soon from *The Refractive Thinker*®
AVAILABLE THRU THE LENTZ LEADERSHIP INSTITUTE

The Refractive Thinker®: *Volume XII: Cybersecurity*

Coming in Summer 2017. The Refractive Thinker® series celebrates the contributions of those involved in the forefront of cybersecurity. From around the globe, scholars offer solution-driven doctoral research that outlines specific and unique contributions of those seeking ever-improving ways to protect our vital informational resources from theft and abuse.

Retailing for $18.95 under the category of Business & Economics/Leadership publications.

For more information, please visit our website: www.RefractiveThinker.com

Other Volumes of *The Refractive Thinker®*

The Refractive Thinker®: Volume I:
An Anthology of Higher Learning

The title of this book, *The Refractive Thinker®*, was chosen intentionally to highlight the ability of these doctoral scholars to bend thought, to converge its very essence on the ability to obliquely pass through the perspective of another. The goal is to ask and ponder the right questions; to dare to think differently, to find new applications within unique and cutting-edge dimensions, ultimately to lead where others may follow or to risk forging perhaps an entirely new path.

The Refractive Thinker®: Volume II:
Research Methodology

The authors within these pages are on a mission to change the world, never satisfied or quite content with what is or asking *why*, instead these authors intentionally strive to push and test the limits to ask *why not*. *The Refractive Thinker®* is an intimate expression of who we are—the ability to think beyond the traditional boundaries of thinking and critical thinking. Instead of mere reflection and evaluation, one challenges the very boundaries of the constructs itself.

For more information, please visit our website: www.RefractiveThinker.com

The Refractive Thinker®: Volume II:
Research Methodology, 2nd Edition

As in Volume I, the authors within these pages are on a mission to change the world, never satisfied or quite content with what is or asking *why*, instead these authors intentionally strive to push and test the limits to ask *why not*. *The Refractive Thinker®* is an intimate expression of who we are—the ability to think beyond the traditional boundaries of thinking and critical thinking. Instead of mere reflection and evaluation, one challenges the very boundaries of the constructs itself.

Chosen as Finalist, Education/Academic category
The USA "Best Books 2011" Awards,
sponsored by USA Book News

The Refractive Thinker®: Volume II:
Research Methodology, 3rd Edition

If thinking is inside the box, and critical thinking is outside the box, refractive thinking is beyond the box. The Refractive Thinker® series provides doctoral scholars with a collaborative opportunity to promote and publish their work in a peer reviewed publication. Our goal is to provide an affordable outlet for scholars that supports the tremendous need for dynamic dialogue and innovation while providing clout and recognition for each.

Winner in the 2013 Global Ebook "Non-Fiction Anthology" category; Finalist, the USA "Best Books 2013" Award; and eLit Bronze 2014 winner

For more information, please visit our website: www.RefractiveThinker.com

The Refractive Thinker®: Volume III: Change Management

This next offering in the series shares yet another glimpse into the scholarly works of these authors, specifically on the topic of change management. In addition to exploring various aspects of change management, the purpose of *The Refractive Thinker®* is also to serve the tenets of leadership. Leadership is not simply a concept outside of the self, but comes from within, defining our very essence; where the search to define leadership becomes our personal journey, not yet a finite destination.

2010 Next Generation Indie Book Awards Finalist

2011 Next Generation Indie Book Awards Finalist

The Refractive Thinker®: Volume IV: Ethics, Leadership, and Globalization

The purpose of this volume is to highlight the scholarly works of these authors on the topics of ethics, leadership, and concerns within the global landscape of business. Join us as we venture forward to showcase the authors of Volume IV, and continue to celebrate the accomplishments of these doctoral scholars affiliated with many phenomenal institutions of higher learning.

Axiom 2011 Bronze Medal • Business Ethics

For more information, please visit our website: www.RefractiveThinker.com

The Refractive Thinker Press Wins 2011 eLit Award for Digital Publishing Excellence

The Refractive Thinker: Vol. V: Strategy in Innovation has been named the winner of the Gold in the Anthology category of the 2011 eLit Awards!

The Refractive Thinker®: Volume VI: Post-Secondary Education

Celebrate the diffusion of innovative refractive thinking through the writings of these doctoral scholars as they dare to think differently in search of new applications and understandings of post-secondary education. Unlike most academic books that merely define research, *The Refractive Thinker®* offers commentary regarding the state of post-secondary education from the perspective of multiple authors—each offering a chapter based on their specific expertise.

For more information, please visit our website: www.RefractiveThinker.com

The Refractive Thinker®: Volume VII: Social Responsibility

The Refractive Thinker® Volume VII, is available to scholars and researchers. The book is part of the multiple award-winning REFRACTIVE THINKER® series published by The Refractive Thinker® Press.

Finalist in the "Anthologies: Non-Fiction" category of the 2013 International Book Awards!

Winner in the "Education/Academic" category, The USA Best Books 2012 Awards, sponsored by USA Book News

The Refractive Thinker®: Volume VIII: Effective Practices for Motivation and Communication

The Spring 2014 release of the Refractive Thinker® anthology marks a new direction for the publication. While previous editions have been curated from a purely academic standpoint, Volume VIII makes the real world connection by bridging the gap. Academicians identify and address the issues in each chapter and Dr. Cheryl Lentz, The Academic Entrepreneur™, provides an interpretation for application into today's business world.

This volume is a true bridge between scholarship and the business community.

Finalist in the 2014 USA Best Book Awards in the "Education/Academic" category.
2015 Next Generation Indie Book Awards Finalist

For more information, please visit our website: www.RefractiveThinker.com

The Refractive Thinker®: Volume IX:
Effective Business Practices
in Leadership & Emerging Technologies

The Refractive Thinker® Volume IX, is available to scholars and researchers. While previous editions have been curated from a purely academic standpoint, Volume IX continues building on the real world connection by bridging the gap. Academicians identify and address the issues in each chapter and provide an interpretation for application into today's business world.

Digital Only: $9.95. Under Business & Economics/Leadership publications.

The Refractive Thinker®: Volume X:
Effective Business Strategies for the
Defense Industry Sector

Join **General Ronald R. Fogleman** and contributing scholars as they discuss research regarding effective business strategies for the defense sector. The conversations include discussions regarding the struggles of a nation to define the way forward regarding the impacts of Defense procurement, Defense health care spending, economic impacts on veteran owned businesses and succession planning, solutions to manage and lead disasters, economic challenges, reduction of energy costs, and exploration of leadership strategies to drive business practices important to the future of our nation. The goal is this volume is to find innovative solutions for more effective outcomes to drive change.

For more information, please visit our website: www.RefractiveThinker.com

The Refractive Thinker®: Volume XI: Women in Leadership

Join Sally Helgesen and contributing scholars as they discuss research regarding women in leadership. The conversations contain research that will influence how women's leadership is understood and supported in the years ahead. This volume provides fresh insights into mentoring and coaching practices, an examination of the importance of developing a voice, the impact of continued shifts in demographics, and the role of women in specific cultures in articulating a sustainable vision of the future. Such contributions will expand and enrich the programmatic offerings that help speed women on their leadership journeys into the future.

Pensiero Press
WHAT'S NEW

THEY ANSWERED THE CALL
Inspirational Stories from Military Veterans and Their Families

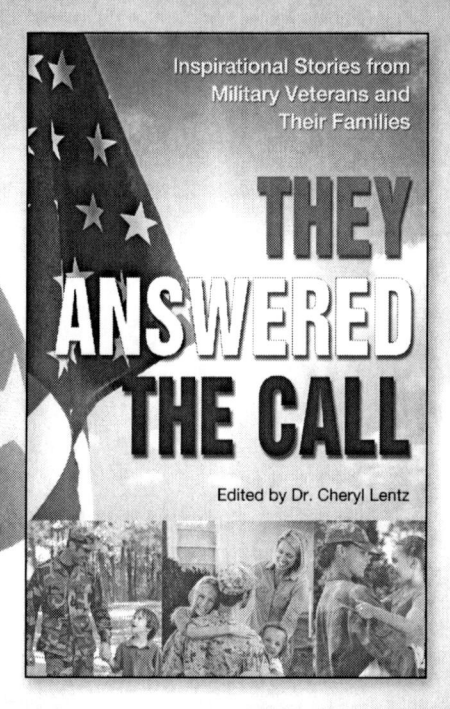

SOMETIMES LEADERSHIP COMES SOFTLY.

A new series of feel-good inspirational stories of hope and humor from active duty military, veterans, and their families. These stories will offer leadership lessons, as well as perseverance through the effective outcomes of challenges that turned into triumphs and victories that everyone can learn from.

Available now. • www.TheyAnsweredTheCall.com

So You Think You Can Edit?
9 Self-Editing Tips for the Novice and Experienced Writer

So You Think You Can Edit? is Dr. Cheryl's most recent book that speaks to the precision of competent writing and editing. She underscores a myriad of practical techniques for validating our choices so we may refine our personal writing acumen, rather than relying on editors to carry the weight. Further, she makes a legitimate case for considering the impressions made when we speak through our articulation and review choices. Each of us, doctorate learner and business executive alike, stands to gain from her insightful guidance.

The Expert Success Solution
Chapter 5—What Would Einstein Do?

Join Dr. Cheryl as she offers proven strategies to shorten your learning curve to think beyond limits when facing problems in your personal and professional settings. Learn to fail faster to succeed sooner using proven skills to move you forward more effectively through individual coaching, Tele Seminars, and online classes using The WRIST Method. Remember, the helping hand you need is at the end of your W-R-I-S-T!

www.ThinkingBeyondLimits.com

The Unbounded Dimensions Series
by Dr. Stephen Hobbs and Dr. Cheryl Lentz

Unbounded Dimensions is a series of ideas, notions, suggestions, inklings, and guesses that the authors believe necessary to challenge mainstream management and leadership thinking and practice. These genius ideas are peripheral concepts and practices with grounded proof of working for the authors and their clients, yet lack mainstay researched exposure upon their presentation in the series. This developmental series enlarges these ideas for others to acknowledge, advance, and amplify in their workplace. In doing so, evidence-based research unfolds within workplaces to confirm or deny the usefulness, worth, and truth of the ideas.

www.UnboundedDimensions.com

Ethics, Employment Law, and Faith-Based Universities: When Law and Faith Collide

What happens when laws change in such a way that violate religious beliefs? This is a question that faith-based universities all over the country have been grappling with since the legalization of same-sex marriage in 2015. This paper attempts to give some guidance and direction to these institutions in applying discrimination laws and to open a dialogue about the ethical obligations to do so.

www.ThePensieroPress.com

PROVEN STUDY TECHNIQUES FROM
Pensiero Press

EFFECTIVE Study Skills
IN **5** SIMPLE STEPS

Dr. Cheryl Lentz has compiled the valuable information she gives in her blog in one easy-to-use handbook. The study tips are designed to help any student improve learning and understanding, and ultimately earn higher grades. The handbook is not so large that it requires long hours of reading, as is the case with many books on the subject. The information is written in a manner to help a learner "see" and "practice" proven study techniques. Effective study skills must be practiced to for improvement to occur.

www.ThePensieroPress.com

TECHNOLOGY THAT TUTORS:
7 Ways to Save Time by Using the Blog as a Teaching Tool

University professors seem to have the same conversation with different students time after time. What if we could be available to our students whenever and wherever we're needed, virtually?

Technology offers such a solution with the creation of the blog. Think of it as technology that tutors 24/7. Welcome to the world of the blog where some of our efforts as professors are now scalable. Learn how you can create a video (with transcript), embed it on your blog, and simply provide the link to your students as the need or topic may arise in class discussions.

Please join me on this journey as I offer a path to shorten your learning curve with increased efficiency in teaching methods as we look to the blog with seven ways to save time by using the blog as a teaching tool.   Visit www.TechnologyThatTutors.com.

WELCOME HOME:
Siberian Husky Rescue Handbook
11 Tips to Welcome a Siberian Rescue into Your Family

Welcome to the Siberian Husky Rescue of New Mexico, Inc. Handbook for new Siberian owners.

Our goal for creating this book is to help new owners prepare themselves for welcoming their newest Siberian Husky rescue into their home. Making a decision to rescue can be one of the most rewarding decisions of a family IF everyone is well prepared. Proceeds benefit this 501c3 rescue group.

This book is written by the founder of Siberian Husky Rescue of New Mexico, International Best Selling Author, Speaker, and Professor, Dr. Cheryl Lentz.

Visit www.DrCherylLentz.com/Siberian-Husky-Rescue

Pensiero Press PUBLISHES LANDMARK BOOK ON THE CHANGING ADULT EDUCATION ARENA

2012 Next Generation Indie Book Awards Finalist

PENSIERO PRESS WINS FINALIST AWARD

May 12, 2012, Las Vegas, NV—*The Consumer Learner* has been named a Finalist in the Education/Academic category of the 2012 Next Generational Indie Book Awards and winner of the 2012 USA Best Book Awards!

Anyone who has entered a college classroom in the last 5 years has recognized a clear transformation in the context of higher education. A dynamic revolution in practice and delivery is underway, and the implications of change are ripe for analysis.

Administrators are increasingly charged with revenue production and institutional leadership. Faculty are experimenting with new models and advances in technology. Students are embracing new modalities as they strive to make curriculum immediately transferable into industry. *The Consumer Learner: Emergence and Expectations of a Customer Service Mentality in Post-Secondary Education* examines the new reality and emerging patterns shaping the experiences of these three diverse, yet interconnected, constituencies.

This book provides a distinctive approach to the transformation of the higher education culture within the U.S. Authors Dr. Gillian Silver and Dr. Cheryl Lentz, noted content experts, professors and curriculum/program developers, explain that the contents will initiate an intensive dialogue about the implications and impacts on administrative structure, faculty practice, and learner outcomes. Says Lentz, "This is a frank, encompassing work that has the capacity to ignite a national dialogue. We think the review will give voice to the significance of this evolving environment. The voices of experience leading this change will emerge."

Follow the authors on the Web: www.consumerlearner.com
and Blog: www.consumerlearner.com/wordpress/

Available through Pensiero Press, a division of the The Lentz Leadership Institute. $24.95 (HARDCOVER)

FROM THE LENTZ LEADERSHIP INSTITUTE

JOURNEY OUTSIDE THE GOLDEN PALACE

DR. CHERYL LENTZ

Come take a mythical journey with Henry from *The Village of Yore* and the many colorful characters of The Golden Palace on their quest to unlock the palatial gates of corporate Ivory Towers. This allegorical tale demonstrates the lessons learned when leaders in organizations fail to serve the needs of their stakeholders. Come join us in a journey toward understanding the elegant simplicity of effective leadership, unlocking the secrets to The Golden Palace Theory of Management along the way.

This revised second edition offers a companion workbook for discussion, reflection, and refractive thinking. Its purpose is to let the reader more closely examine each character and their leadership qualities. Take a leap of faith and follow us on our journey. Perhaps you may recognize some old friends on your travels.

www.ThePensieroPress.com

PUBLICATIONS ORDER FORM

Please send the following books:
- [ ] *The Refractive Thinker®: Volume I: An Anthology of Higher Learning*
- [ ] *The Refractive Thinker®: Volume II: Research Methodology*
- [ ] *The Refractive Thinker®: Volume II: Research Methodology, 2nd Edition*
- [ ] *The Refractive Thinker®: Volume II: Research Methodology, 3rd Edition*
- [ ] *The Refractive Thinker®: Volume III: Change Management*
- [ ] *The Refractive Thinker®: Volume IV: Ethics, Leadership, and Globalization*
- [ ] *The Refractive Thinker®: Volume V: Strategy in Innovation*
- [ ] *The Refractive Thinker®: Volume VI: Post-Secondary Education*
- [ ] *The Refractive Thinker®: Volume VII: Social Responsibility*
- [ ] *The Refractive Thinker®: Volume VIII: Effective Business Practices*
- [ ] *The Refractive Thinker®: Volume IX: Effective Business Practices in Leadership & Emerging Technologies*
- [ ] *The Refractive Thinker®: Volume X: Effective Business Strategies for the Defense Industry Sector*
- [ ] *The Refractive Thinker®: Volume XI: Women in Leadership*

Please contact the Refractive Thinker® Press for book prices, e-book prices, and shipping. Individual e-chapters available by author: $3.95 (plus applicable tax). www.RefractiveThinker.com

- [ ] *They Answered the Call*
- [ ] *So You Think You Can Edit?*
- [ ] *The Expert Success Solution*
- [ ] *The Unbounded Dimensions Series*
- [ ] *Ethics, Employment Law, and Faith-Based Universities*
- [ ] *Effective Study Skills in 5 Simple Steps*
- [ ] *Technology That Tutors*
- [ ] *Siberian Husky Rescue*
- [ ] *The Consumer Learner*
- [ ] *Journey Outside the Golden Palace*

Please send more FREE information and join our mailing list:
- [ ] Speaking engagements
- [ ] Educational seminars
- [ ] Consulting

Name: _____

Address: _____

City: _____ State: _____ Zip: _____

Telephone: _____ Email: _____

NM Residents please add 7.187% gross receipts tax • *Please see our website for shipping rates.*

Mail to: The Refractive Thinker® Press/Pensiero Press
7124 Glyndon Trail NW • Albuquerque, NM 87114

Participation in Future Volumes of The Refractive Thinker®

Yes, I would like to participate in:

❏ **Doctoral Volume**(s) for a specific university or organization:

Name: _____

Contact Person: _____

Telephone: _____ E-mail: _____

❏ **Specialized Volume**(s) Business or Themed:

Name: _____

Contact Person: _____

Telephone: _____ E-mail: _____

Please mail or e-mail form to:

The Refractive Thinker® Press
7124 Glyndon Trail NW
Albuquerque, NM 87114 USA

www.RefractiveThinker.com

Join us on Twitter, LinkedIn, and Facebook